How to
STAND UP
and SPEAK WELL
in Business

BUSINESS MEETING . . .
COMPANY DINNER. . . .
CLIENT PRESENTATION. . . .
BUDGET MEETING. . . .
SALES CONVENTION. . . .
MARKETING REVIEW. . . .

President, salesman, executive, trainee—your position will grow when you speak.

STAND UP and speak well!

How to
STAND UP
and SPEAK WELL
in Business

by FRANK SNELL

CORNERSTONE LIBRARY • NEW YORK

CORNERSTONE LIBRARY PUBLICATIONS
are distributed by
Simon & Schuster, Inc.
630 Fifth Avenue
New York, New York 10020
Manufactured in the United States of America
under the supervision of
Rolls Offset Printing Co., N.Y.

"*If all my possessions were taken from me with one exception, I would choose to keep the power of speech, for by it I would soon regain all the rest.*"

DANIEL WEBSTER

CONTENTS

Foreword

This book was written with one very clear goal in view. It was written to make you a more interesting, compelling, authoritative and valuable person in front of your listeners. It is specifically designed to make you a good business speaker.

You do not need to be told the value of speaking well. If you have been asked to make a speech or expect to be asked, you are fully aware of the problem. Anyone who has stood before an audience to speak his ideas knows the room there is for improvement.

To be able to stand up and speak well is a part of our everyday life in business. In spite of the flood of memos and letters that cross the businessman's desk, they represent only a trickle in his everyday communications. The printed word simply cannot handle the job. For over ninety percent of our ideas are spoken. Speech is truly everybody's business!

I have worked with hundreds of businessmen who needed to speak on their feet; men in business, in industry, in advertising, in science. Men who came to Columbia

University's School of General Studies, men who would break away for an hour to work with the author in the privacy of their office, men who would give up their lunch to take a company-sponsored class. All men who recognized that their future depended ultimately on their ability to communicate their ideas with the spoken word.

Speaking techniques have not leaped forward as the sciences have in recent years. Speaking has not moved as has flight from Kitty Hawk to Cape Canaveral, from 120 feet to a projected 900 million miles to Saturn. It has not made these fantastic jumps, but it remains more important than any of them. It remains humanity's irreplaceable tool for progress. We could live our daily lives without rockets; we cannot live without speech—a fact we all rediscover daily.

Learning to speak well demands more than the desire of the speaker to do so. Forceful, vital speaking in business comes with an understanding of what good speaking is and how *you* can make it part of your business life. It calls for knowing what the audience wants to hear and what it automatically rejects. It calls for a polishing of your speaking tools . . . words, structure, logic.   It calls for using those abilities that makes one man stand out from the rest.

And this is what this book will show you . . . How to stand out from the rest!

FRANK SNELL

First Principles

Lᴇᴛ'ꜱ ꜱᴛᴀᴛᴇ an important point as simply as possible! This statement will serve to clear the air of harmful misconceptions that drift into the thinking of prospective speakers and severely limit their speaking improvement.

First, speaking in public is not easy for *most* people!

Standing in front of an audience to speak ideas with directness, ease and persuasion has troubled men for centuries. It probably troubles you. You are *not alone!*

It would be nice to be able to say that the usual feelings of inadequacy, awkwardness, fear and trembling can be overcome by some magic elixir, some mystical incantation.

Unfortunately, this is not possible. You would be wasting your time looking for an enchanted path to successful speaking. It does not exist!

There is no quick and easy road. There is no glib formula, no slick equation or pat terminology. You have to *work at* becoming a good speaker.

Napoleon was once asked by a visiting diplomat if he would name the most essential ingredient of success. Was it genius? Was it personal drive? Was it follow-through, or perhaps leadership?

Napoleon never hesitated. His answer was direct and simple: "Practice, practice, practice!"

Keep this answer in mind. It is also the secret of good speaking.

You . . . and Your Speaking

IF THIS BOOK does have a secret to tell, it's this: You can *learn* to speak effectively. This means everyone!

You don't expect to walk up to a tee and drive a ball 250 yards without practice. You don't expect to drop a fly in that black pool behind a log from twenty yards out without practice. You don't expect to step up and bowl a 200 average your first week at the alleys.

If you do, you're fooling yourself . . . and you should know it better than anyone else!

You have to *learn* to do these things. You learn to swim; learn to drive a car. You learn to write, read, dance, bowl, grow flowers, a thousand and one other things. You can learn to speak well!

What this book will give you is a blueprint to good speaking. A plan that will tell you the *right* things to learn; tell you what is important and what you needn't worry about. It will show you how to analyze and evaluate your speaking, and to recognize someone else's good speech when you hear it. It will tell you what an audience wants to hear; and how much. It will warn you when you have said enough and when to sit down.

Most important of all, it will tell you how to do these things with force and effectiveness.

Now let's start with the first basic rule . . . the foundation of *everything* to follow.

This book was written for *you!* Don't ever doubt that *you* can be a good speaker!

Speech and Today's Business World

THE SPEAKER . . . the businessman . . . the salesman . . . the committee member . . . the executive . . . the company president . . . you. All with the same problem . . . and opportunity. You and your ability to speak are forever tied together and will to a great degree determine your future in your business life.

As long as you live, you are going to have to get along with words. You're going to have to choose them, weigh them, read them, write them. Most important of all, you are going to have to speak them.

Today's world, more than ever before, is based on the communication of ideas, concepts, feelings, plans, arguments, facts. The sciences, philosophy, religion—all depend equally on the spoken word for their life and growth. Without this communication, the building and passing of knowledge would be slow indeed.

The spoken word has been a vital carrier of knowledge in all ages; a far greater force than printed material. It is speech, not fire, that has made man greater than the animals.

It is readily accepted that today's businessman must be the master of his words and of the techniques of presenting them. Everyday you must pass on to your friends your thoughts, feelings, decisions. In your conversation your friends and colleagues really get to know you. Through your speaking, they are also able to know *what* you know. You owe it to yourself to give yourself the best possible break; don't let weak speaking habits tell false tales about your ability. Let your speech underline your clarity of thinking, directness, decisiveness. Make your speaking *work* for you.

How much does speech count? Let's see. The average man speaks about 30,000 words a day. Let's say about 3,100 words an hour through the normal working day. It doesn't take much insight to see that the spoken word is with you constantly; that it is a continuing good advertisement for you and your work, if you make it so.

The Speaker

BRUCE BARTON, one of America's great advertising men, once made this searching comment:

"In my library are about a thousand volumes of biography. A rough calculation indicates that more of these deal with men who have talked their way upward than with all the scientists, writers, saints, and doers combined. The talkers have always ruled. The smart thing is to join them."

The point is well made. Mr. Barton is not endorsing the demagogue, individuals who move audiences to base deeds; men like Hitler, Mussolini, Stalin. Mr. Barton is pleading for men with good ideas to prepare themselves to take hold and exert their knowledge and leadership.

Mr. Barton is stating what all business leaders know. Effective speaking is no luxury in today's business world. It's a necessity! It goes hand in hand with growth and responsibility. To join the talkers is obviously the thing to do. The question remains . . . how?

Let's try to answer this question now.

The first ingredient for an effective, direct, forceful speech is the speaker himself. He is the single indispensable factor who will always remain the center post around which any speech will revolve. Make the speaker more adaptable and responsive to his role and the first *big* step has been taken in the direction of good speaking.

What is it that causes such a violent change in an individual who is called upon to stand in front of an audience and present his thoughts? Why does the normally intelligent person suddenly become gray; stumble; act like a trapped animal? What makes him lose his thoughts and throw away just those ideas that he knows best; those ideas that are part of his everyday thinking and work?

These are questions about the speaker that must be answered. These answers will start speakers on the road to speaking success. These are answers we will seek to find immediately.

Stage Fright

"Oh wad some power the giftie gie us
To see oursels as others see us."

ROBERT BURNS

THERE IS a clue in this statement by the most famous of all Scottish poets that can help make you a better speaker. If we can understand ourselves better, particularly in the speaking situation, we will soon know how to overcome the feelings of fear and uncertainty that everyone experiences when he *stands up* to talk. "Stand up" is stressed because this is what makes this type of speaking different and more difficult than everyday casual talking with your fellow workers and friends.

Why does stage fright exist? Let's see.

For most of us, conversation with friends is a natural and pleasant experience. Yet this *same* talk on the *same* subjects in front of an audience seems unnatural and disagreeable. Why? The answer can be found in that one *added* factor; the changed *position* of the speaker.

Look at it this way. The speaker experiences little pressure in everyday conversation. He is rarely "under the gun." He knows that if he wishes, he may at any time step right out of the speech situation and remove himself completely from any responsibility in carrying on the conversation. This type of communicating is strictly informal and places the emphasis and attention of the speaker exactly where it should be—on passing information.

Unfortunately, this is not the case in talking before an audience, regardless of whether the audience is big or small, friendly or foreign.

When the speaker stands on his feet to talk to a group of listeners, he *knows* that he is there until the end of his speech. He knows he has committed himself to a formal presentation of ideas, and he has taken on himself the *full* responsibility!

This, of course, should be expected. The speaker should and must assume full responsibility in making a speech. But still the question needs to be answered, "Why does this change of position make well-adjusted, normal people turn pale and wilt"

The answer is no deep, dark secret. A moment's examination clearly spotlights the cause of the speaker's dilemma; the common cause of all stage fright.

Man, like all other animals, is governed by a powerful desire to be part of the group. He lives in a family, a community, a club, a company, a country, etc. All his activities are made up of being part of a larger unit working together and mutually supporting one another. Any activity that works counter to this pattern, which does not seem to trade on the contributions of the group, is strange to the existence of the individual. Simply stated, it is very hard for a person to "go it alone"; and this is what the speaker feels he is being asked to do when he stands in front of an audience.

Think for a minute how hard everyone works to organize his life and work. The businessman looks for a good job, gets it, and then works to increase his value to his company. In return, he receives security, prestige, continuing growth and responsibility. The future looks rosy!

Then comes the big bugaboo—the request that he make a speech! With this the big fear comes to light; the fear the speaker has of showing up poorly, that this performance could risk all the prestige gained by years of hard work. All thrown away in one brief moment. The chips are down!

This single fear makes speaking ten times more difficult than it ever need be.

Let's look even more closely at this dilemma and see what other reasons make talking in front of an audience so much more difficult than everyday casual conversation with friends.

First, in conversation all the participating members are equal; they are *all* speakers; no one is on the spot. Without this focus of responsibility, the tension on the individual member is *greatly* reduced.

When you *stand* in front of a group to present your ideas, there is only *one* speaker, only one person who bears *all* the responsibility for the conversation . . . *you*. As speaker, you are bound to feel this responsibility deeply. This sense of pressure results in tension and fear!

Second, in conversation, the speaker can stop participating almost at will. There are always others who will pick up conversing where he leaves off. Chances are that they will all be straining to get into the act, anxious to say their piece. This makes the conversational speaker's task relatively easy.

In conversation, the conversationalist can gauge his effectiveness by the comments of the other speakers. This gives him an accurate and running measure of the effect his words are having on his listeners.

Think for a moment how hard it is to talk to someone who is reluctant to talk back. Someone who does not respond to any of your statements; refuses to answer your questions; will not give approval *or* disapproval. Would you know where you were; whether your ideas were getting through? Of course not. Is it any wonder that when this happens to you as you stand before an andience you soon begin to feel awkward and ill at ease? Pretty soon you begin to think of those long pauses; you begin to wonder just what your listeners are thinking. Soon the whole speech begins to rattle, seems to break down.

The speaker would like to have someone tell him that he is doing a good job. He'd like to have someone respond to the ideas he's presenting. Unfortunately, he has made one basic mistake. He has overlooked one important fact. It is not the audience's *place* to talk back! They know it, and you as a speaker should too.

Therefore, don't mistake the silence of the audience for hostility. Don't allow the appearance of all those eyes staring at you lead you to believe they are thirsting for your failure. This is just not so.

This look at the speaker in conversation and the speaker on his feet before a group is *very* important. Remember it as you move ahead, it will help you understand your audience better and assist you in getting them to work *for* you.

Getting to know your audience and learning to understand your feelings when you stand before them represents a giant step down the road to being a better speaker. The following pages will help you take that step.

The Positive Approach
to Your Audience

MOST ANYONE who has stood before an audience will tell you he felt that twinge of apprehension as he walked out onto the platform. He will also tell you that this is not something that disappears after the first few speaking experiences. In fact, with most speakers, this wave of excitement will continue to be a normal part of the speaking situation.

However, as pointed out earlier, this is a natural reaction in the human being; a sign that he is stepping out of the mold and doing something important and different. The important thing is that the speaker recognize what is happening and treat it as the expected.

If you want a good rule of thumb for helping to overcome the fear of stage fright, it's this: Don't expect the situation to be natural. Don't expect to feel at ease. Don't look for relaxation in a situation in which it just doesn't exist!

Instead, direct your energies in other more profitable direction. Ones that can *really* pay off!

George Bernard Shaw, the famous Irish playwright and critic, constantly stated his belief in the power of facing reality; of the strength that can be gained by standing up and meeting a situation face to face. He said, "The people who got on in this world, are the people who get up and look for the circumstances they want, and, if they can't find them, make them."

The speaker can use this bit of advice. He can make it work directly for him; use it as a guide to facing the problem of standing up to an audience.

The speaker normally feels insecure. Granted. What can he do about it? Here's a check list!

——ATTACK THE SITUATION POSITIVELY

——STAND UP TO YOUR AUDIENCE

——FORCE YOUR AUDIENCE TO CONVERSE WITH YOU

——MAKE THE AUDIENCE KNOW YOU EXPECT TO SUCCEED

——SPEAK OUT WITH AUTHORITY

——GESTURE

Easy to say, you may think, but lots more difficult to do! Strangely enough, it is not really difficult at all. The most difficult part has already been overcome by you when you read the above listed ideas. The difficult part is to get the ideas clearly in mind . . . *and* to be willing to make the effort to make them work! Let's take them one by one.

ATTACK THE SITUATION POSITIVELY

Horace, the poet of the golden era of Rome, wisely

pointed out that: "He who makes a good start, has half the job done."

He couldn't have been more right, and the good start in any speech is in the preparation. Prepare! For this there is no substitute. Don't make your task doubly difficult; preparation is the biggest gun in your arsenal. If, as the Duke of Wellington said, the battle of Waterloo was won with the manliness and courage the English had developed on the playing fields of Eton, your speech battle will be won in the time and effort you give yourself to prepare!

You cannot expect to give a good speech if you don't have one ready and primed to flow out. You can't just stand up and speak coherently and directly on the spur of the moment. You *can* be sure that many speaking failures have thought that preparation was a luxury and decided to risk a one-shot performance.

Evaluate the importance of that one speaking chance. You can only agree it's worth the preparation.

Rise to your audience positively! Walk definitely and stand solidly. Face them securely. This is your chance to take the reins; your chance to control your listeners; your first chance to make your own job easier.

It is important to remember that as speaker your every movement and action will be carefully watched and evaluated by your audience. You have assumed a position of importance; as speaker you have taken a position the audience recognizes as important.

They naturally want to know as much about you as they can in the very short time you will be in front of them. This is an audience made up of individuals, and one of the known desires of individuals is the urge to know about and understand a situation faster than the surrounding group. As speaker, you are a "personality"; personalities are always carefully watched and admired. Learn to accept this honor! This heightened interest accounts for the audience's appearance of examining critically every speaker that stands before them.

This should not be interpreted as a desire to see you make tragic mistakes!

However, remember your actions *are* being watched and your speech *will* be judged in no small part by the way you approach your listeners.

If you seem stunned by the tension of the situation, your audience will be so disturbed they won't hear what you have to say. If you show yourself reluctant to take the position of speaker, they will deny you the authority that goes with that position. If you stumble and apologize, your listeners will begin to question your knowledge of the subject. With this questioning invariably comes a doubt of whether the speaker is worth listening to at all!

The weak approach to the audience has been the death-knell of a multitude of well-meaning but uninformed public speakers!

Your job has been defined—as speaker your role of leader has been set up.

Be that person!

STAND UP TO YOUR AUDIENCE

Emerson, the American philosopher of the nineteenth century, once said, "What you are thunders so loud, I can't hear what you say."

He was underlining what thousands of articulate audiences will quickly tell you. They just can't divorce how a speaker acts from what he says. The two are inexorably tied together. *Rule:* Look the part of the speaker . . . be assured and make every effort to take control. Be your best self. Command the situation. Audiences like firmness.

Stand firmly before the audience. Place your feet about twelve inches apart and look as though you are on the attack, not retreating. This will help you look the part of the leader. Distribute your weight evenly on both feet. Don't sway from side to side or shift from foot to foot. This "rumba technique" can only serve to make your audience wonder whether they have come to hear a speech or to go on an ocean voyage.

Let your hands hang easily at your sides. Better still, gesture! Gestures give you something to do with your hands and will make you look and feel more at ease. One thing *not* to do with your hands is to let them jingle coins or keys. This is one of the pet peeves of audiences. They would much rather the speaker count his money in the more appropriate quiet of his own home. Experienced speakers will confirm that this is one of the surest ways of throwing your listeners away!

When you step up to make your presentation, face your audience, pause for attention, take command, let yourself go. The control rests with you.

FORCE YOUR AUDIENCE TO CONVERSE WITH YOU

To step from conversation to public speaking, from friends to audience, from few to many, is to step naturally from the simple to the more difficult. We've already discussed the difference. One question remains: "Can the ease with which we are able to take part in conversation help us in public speaking?"

Certainly! The same basic principle governs both.

First, realize that your speech, presented though it is before an audience, *is* a conversation. It is simply conversation in an expanded form. Except for the increased projection of your voice, the change from an audience of two to an audience of two hundred should not materially change the style or manner of your delivery.

To be effective, the speaker must constantly be concerned with the conversational contact of speaker and audience. It is perhaps the most concrete tie he can maintain with the listener. Trade on it. Always be sure you are *conversing with*, not *talking at*, an audience.

Naturally, in this "conversation" your audience can't talk back, won't join in vocally. They know it would be impolite to break in on this speech situation. They know they should give you their undivided attention and profit by catching every word.

As a matter of fact, there are very few gestures of approval that the audience *can* make. You wouldn't really expect them to wave their arms or stamp their feet. At least not in response to the usual speech. They know it would just serve to embarrass you . . . and them.

Conversing with your audience is not, of course, only vocal; it is also a physical activity. One of the basic requirements of every speaker is that he *look at* his listeners as he would if he were in conversation. This physical meeting of speaker and listener is usually referred to as "eye contact."

Again, the parallel of the speech and conversation is clear. How many times have you heard someone say "I like a person who looks at me when he talks." This is expected of anyone who wishes to present an appearance of honesty, dependability and security; the very attributes most important to a speaker since these attributes are among the first to be searched out by every audience. They want to see if these signs of honesty and stability are present in their speaker. If they are, the listener will find it much easier to accept what he has to say. If they are not, the speaker has very little chance of success.

This brings up two very common, but nonetheless false ideas you frequently get from misinformed speakers. They are: "I find that if I look out of the window, I can clear my mind for a moment. Then perhaps I can remember what I was going to say." Or, "If I look over the head of the last man in the audience, all my listeners will think I'm looking directly at them."

Pure rationalizing! These old wives' tales have done nothing but perpetuate a long line of ineffective, boring speakers.

The only reason speakers look out of the window is because they want to escape from their audience. To look into the deep gloom in the back of the hall is still another attempt to avoid the eyes of the listeners.

Face up to the speech situation. Don't try to avoid your role as speaker. Your ideas must flow in one direction—from you *straight* to your listeners. Let your eyes help you. Let them serve as a firm handshake with your audience. Let them tell your audience that you are a person they can trust and believe.

One final suggestion. Spread your eye contact around. Look at different listeners in your audience. If it's a large group, pick individuals in different parts of the hall. Don't leave any area out; the people there will naturally feel slighted and you may very well lose their support.

Be sure, of course, you are really looking at your listeners as you would a friend you were talking to on the street or in your home. Don't just flash a glassy stare.

When you turn from one part of the audience to another, turn your head. Avoid the furtive glance out of the corners of your eyes. This gives you a shifty, untrustworthy look. An audience that doesn't trust you won't ever believe what you have to say.

These principles will help you in your speaking if you will always use them. They will certainly help you get your audience to like you as a speaker. If they like you, they will listen. If they listen, they may believe you. One thing you can count on—if you don't use them, your chance of giving a good speech is small indeed!

MAKE YOUR AUDIENCE KNOW YOU EXPECT TO SUCCEED

The comic salesman who stands at your door and says, "You probably wouldn't be interested in buying this brush, would you?" is doomed before he begins. The same is true of the speaker who seems to make every effort to prove to his audience that they probably have heard anything he might have to say, and they probably wouldn't believe it anyway! The effective speaker *must* be convinced that he has something important to tell his listeners and this conviction must be carried over to the audience in his every word and action. Obviously, there is very little room for the speaker who has convinced himself that he simply doesn't want to speak!

Recognize that you really want to succeed. Then prove this to your audience by showing you know your subject is important, and that you are willing to make the effort to convince them of your point of view.

Remember this: All the chance for success lies in your hands. *You* have the full opportunity to interest your listeners and to lead them to your conclusions. *You* hold the power to move them to action. You are working with a powerful force . . . the spoken word. Listen to the judgment of Joseph Conrad, the great English novelist. He said there was nothing to equal its power: "Give me the right word, and I'll move the world."

Too many speakers fail to understand the strength of the medium they are using. It isn't enough to think, "Well, I'll get through the speech somehow." The getting through is nothing! It isn't even worth making a speech for! *Anyone* can get through. The important goal is to try to give your listeners something of value in a direct, clear, timesaving form; to help them see a subject better than they ever did before.

This is a worthwhile goal!

Let your audience know you plan to succeed and it will make it easier for them to receive what you have to say.

SPEAK WITH AUTHORITY

Three hundred and fifty years ago, William Shakespeare, the greatest master of the word who ever lived, warned, "Look to your speech, lest it mar your fortune." The Elizabethan speaker with a thin, nervous, weak voice could expect the same response from his audience as the speaker today—a refusal to listen or believe.

The man who wants to be a good speaker, wants to direct the thinking of his listeners, can't afford weak, faulty equipment. His voice must reinforce and complement his direct and authoritative appearance; it must be full and firm.

Speak out! Be sure you can be heard by everyone; particularly the last man in the last row. He is frequently the forgotten man in audiences. Open your mouth and let the words form freely and fully. Breathe deeply and project your voice. Watch your pacing and timing. Practice speaking aloud; make your family listen. Your voice is a tremendously valuable property. Develop it.

To sum up: Your voice and your physical appearance *plus* your positive attitude must *all* work together to tell your audience, "I have something to tell you that is worthwhile. Something that will help you and inform you if you listen. I plan to present it directly, clearly and easily. Listen carefully. You'll be glad you did!"

One final but vital idea: Give yourself completely to your speaking. *Want* to give a good speech and be prepared to make the *full* effort. Benefit from the advice of Terence, a Roman playwright of 2100 years ago: "There is nothing so easy but that it becomes difficult when done with reluctance."

GESTURES

Specialists in the study of language tell us that speech is simply gesture made audible; that speech is gesture that can be *listened to* instead of watched.

There can be no doubt that gesture came earlier in man's development than speech. Gesture carried men through those long dark ages of the beginning of mankind until the time humans learned to form sound symbols. Gestures are still an essential tool of the speaker.

Unfortunately, most beginning speakers find it very hard to learn to gesture.

One of the chronic questions asked by speakers is, "What do I do with my hands?" This sounds like a reasonable question. But in fact, it isn't! What the speaker usually means is, "How can I make my hands less conspicuous? How can I hide those troublesome objects that are attached to the ends of my arms?" No speaker ever profited by trying to solve this question! Turn over the coin; look at it from the *other* side!

Ask, "How can I make my hands support my speaking?" The answer to *this* question is available and it can help you tremendously!

Some of us talk with our hands naturally; others of us do not. Therefore, some will have to work harder to master the technique. But this is true of everything we do. The results of this effort are more than worth the trying.

Here are some suggestions:

First, keep your hands out of your pockets. It isn't a question of good manners, just a question of good sense. The temptation to play with keys and coins and other paraphernalia is too great for most speakers. More than that, with your hands in your pockets, you will *never* learn to gesture.

Talk with your hands; make them describe, clarify, amplify, spotlight the ideas your words present. Show the size of objects, point to things, gesture to show importance.

In short, use your hands to *show* your ideas.

The following are some basic rules for the use of gestures

to support your speaking:

1. About 90% of all gestures should be made above the waist. Gestures made below the waist indicate failure, defeat, despair.

2. Keep your forearms roughly parallel to the waist, with your elbows about three inches from your sides. Elbows too close to the body are awkward and tend to symbolize smallness and weaken the authority of the speaker.

3. Don't break your wrists when you gesture. Make your hands part of your forearm. Open your hands and keep the fingers slightly curved; as if you were holding a grapefruit. Lax hands can indicate a lack of power and therefore lack of leadership by the speaker.

4. Use *both* hands. A speaker who always gestures with only one hand is like a car running on three cylinders . . . you're glad you're getting something out of it, but it doesn't provide the power you would hope for! Use both hands and be a fully operating speaker.

The most difficult part of learning to gesture is to get started, to begin to use gestures you feel are not erratic, awkward, unnecessary. Since using your hands to speak is very much part of the personality of every individual, it is difficult to put gestures in categories.

The following will, however, help define the *types* of gestures you can use, and give you material for practice and development.

Here are the three basic kinds of gestures all speakers can put to use:

1. Gestures of direction
2. Gestures of size, shape, and description
3. Gestures of feeling and intensity

And here's how each type occurs in our speaking. In the following examples, the *italicized* words point out where the gestures could be used.

GESTURES OF DIRECTION

"He jumped off *that rock*, and went right *down that hole* near the tree."

"We drove all that night through a *narrow pass*, and in the morning we were *facing that way*."

"*That's our new machine*. Note that it's fully automatic and is controlled by the supervisor from his control panel *on that first landing*."

"*Go down that road*. On your left, you'll see a red barn, *turn down* into the hollow and there's the house.

"*You* know it, and *I* know it. If we want our business to *go up*, we must modernize our equipment."

GESTURES OF SIZE, SHAPE AND DESCRIPTION

"There in the bottom of the boat was the *biggest fish* I'd ever caught. But before I could *grab him*, etc. . . ."

"This is *a small wheel*, about the size of a saucer. *On one side, it has teeth* designed to mesh on the shaft."

"*Chop this way*, and you'll find that the wedges will *chip out* easily."

"It wasn't *exactly round*, more *egg-shaped*; we sent up a plane to investigate. He dived through a *huge* cloud, and found . . . nothing."

"The wrapper should be approximately *this wide*, with the *lettering running along the edge*."

GESTURES OF FEELING AND INTENSITY

These gestures are the most difficult to classify, and equally difficult to define as to their use. They are, however, also the type of gesture most used in our attempts to express ourselves more fully and clearly. These gestures show the attitude and mood of the speaker. They tell the listener how the speaker feels about his subject, and the intensity with which he demands a change. They are a thermometer of feelings.

Imagine the speaker, arms extended below the waist, palms out:

> "I have tried to get the people of this town to realize what would happen if we did not built that school, but *I have failed*."

Visualize the speaker, arms extended waist high, his fingers slightly curved, saying,

> "You know how firmly I believe that *we are all in this together; that we should all share in the profits*."

As the arms of the speaker rise, the degree of intensity increases. Imagine the speaker, full of emotion; his arms raised to the sky:

> "*How much, how much are we asked to take?* If we do not drive the racketeers from this city, we

do not have the right to call ourselves citizens!"

Gestures are essential to speaking. When you fail to use them you are placing yourself at a severe disadvantage. They are a fundamental means of communicating ideas; a means that *all* audiences understand.

Be sure you gesture in your next speech. Don't be afraid to make mistakes. If you think of gestures as "talking with your hands," they will come easily. You will soon see that gesture is truly the foundation of language.

The speaker is a walking visual aid. How he looks tells his audience how he thinks.

Look strong, secure, authoritative. Your listener will treat your words the same way.

EXERCISES. . . .

1. List in your mind a dozen 'weak' signs you have seen in other speakers as they approached their audience. What effect do you think they had on the listeners? Why?

2. Stand before a mirror and talk to an imaginary audience. Do you look natural? Are you relaxed? Reason with your listeners, try to convince them to do something, as if you were talking to a friend. Talk about football, the flower show, sailing, anything.

3. Stand in the living room and imagine an audience before you. Spread your 'eye-contact' around. Don't slight any part of the audience. Talk to each section of your audience for a moment.

4. Here are some 'gesture situations'. Make them live for your listeners.

   a. You have lost your keys somewhere in your

car. Show your listeners how you searched everywhere to find them.

b. You were canoeing down a violent river. Describe the rushing water, the pitching of the canoe, the rocks, the frantic paddling. Now describe the calmness of the river and the beauty of the wilderness when you came out of the rapids. Let yourself go!

5. Describe the small details of an object, a lighter, a calculator, a jeweled pin. Turn it over to describe it to your 'audience' in the mirror.

6. Sit down and imagine yourself waiting to be called to speak. Then rise and walk to the front of the stage and speak to that audience. Be relaxed, be strong, be direct. Most of all, be controlled. If you're not satisfied, sit down and approach your audience again.

Don't be satisfied with a weak performance. Approach your audience positively!

The Audience

A FAMOUS seventeenth century playwright vividly described that terrifying mass of listeners known as the audience as follows: "Like hungry guests, a sitting audience looks."

This description made over three hundred years ago is an accurate one and just as familiar to the speaker today as it was then. Audiences haven't changed much! To most speakers, they definitely look hungry! And in one sense, they are! But the common mistake almost all speakers make is to think that the audience is hungry for the scalp of the man standing before them. Nothing could be less profitable for the audience! They *are* hungry . . . , but hungry for information, facts, ideas . . . tied up in the framework of a well-presented speech!

The first chapter pointed out that the speaker rightly feels he is under the gun. He feels that all he has worked for in his business, his community, his social contacts, etc., depends *completely* on how well *this* speech comes off. He feels alone, on trial, set upon by his audience.

As a result of all these understandable, but none the less incorrect thoughts, the speaker looks upon the audience as a many-headed monster! As he *thinks* of the audience in this grim way, he begins to imagine what the audience thinks of *him*. Usually he thinks they want to destroy him; that they want him to fail; just for their frivolous amusement.

He is, of course, in error. Audiences are just not like this!

The fact is the audience is much more sinned against than sinning. There is not a single record in history of this many-headed monster ever devouring a speaker! It simply doesn't think this way. These are just the vivid imaginings of the speaker to compensate for his feelings of insecurity, and lack of confidence.

Since the habits of the average audience are *so* misunderstood, the time will be well spent finding out what it *is* like. Let's examine it closely; you'll find it will help greatly to cut away your basic fears of facing your listeners.

Perhaps you'll find that the writhing and frightening appearance of the audience is not a sign of anger and ferocity, but simply an indication of boredom!

Like any other group of people, the audience can be conditioned, and it has been conditioned for years to expect to be bored by speakers who "Tell stories they can't remember to people who have heard them already."

An interminable number of speakers, over centuries, stuttering endless words, have put out any fire of excitement that might still flicker for people who honestly *like* to listen to a good speech or presentation.

But there is one very important factor for you to remember . . . this fire *can* be relighted! And if *you* do it, it may change your entire future.

Call it the hope that springs eternal! Audiences still hope against hope to hear a good speech given by a good speaker. Perhaps you, as the next speaker, hold the spark!

To do this, you must know your audience intimately. What is the audience like? How about its attitude? How does it feel about the speaker? What does it want from him? Is it dangerous? What are its interests? Is it true that it wants the speaker to fail? Is it really antagonistic? Is it sadistic? You have to examine it to find the answers.

Look at it this way. In any normal cross-section of people, it's the rare exception that takes joy at the discomfort of someone else. This holds true with your audience. It's absurd to think the audience would want to mishandle its speaker. They're humans like you, and they have better things to do than pull the wings off flies!

It's true that the mood of the audience is difficult to describe because of its complexity. There are, however, two basic overriding emotions that guide its thinking.

First, and most important, the audience wants the speaker to speak well. Second, it wants him to sit down.

In the first place, the audience wants sincerely to hear a good, vital speech; a well-directed, concise, interesting speech given with force and sureness. The second emotion, that of wishing the speaker to sit down is a natural one. They want to get through what is being said in a reasonable period and return to their other business activities which call into being their own physical and mental actions. They have unfortunately, seen and heard many speeches and very likely few that have been successfully completed in a reasonable and logical length of time!

The idea that an audience is antagonistic and sadistic is, of course, idiotic. The truth is that it is the *audience* that suffers in too many speech situations. How? Take this as an example.

Picture yourself in a high school auditorium at graduation time. The ceremonies are in full swing. You are relaxed and enjoying the evening. Then you glance at your program! Mary Cummins, that nice little girl next door, is listed as singing an aria from *Aida. Aida!* That's certainly a tough assignment for a youngster! Why in the world would anyone choose to have her do that! Sure, she has a good voice, but . . . ! She couldn't possibly . . . This is too advanced! . . . The poor kid will break. . . .

Your relaxed evening has gone by the boards! The stage is set for the audience-speaker, in this case the audience-singer *worry* relationship. You have been drawn into the normal audience concern about the speaker. You want Mary Cummins to succeed and you are afraid she won't!

The tension for you will continue to grow. You are uneasy. You might analyze your feelings and realize that it is your doubt in her ability that has made you uncomfortable. You might even mutter a short prayer: "Please, this is a rough job this kid has to do. Let her make it just this once."

You are completely on her side . . . but, you *are* uncomfortable.

To Mary, or to a speaker on the platform, your squirming and twisting in your seat could be mistaken for boredom or even just plain antagonism. You can see how wrong the speaker can be in his judgment of his audience. How completely offbase he can be when he thinks his audience *wants* him to fail.

But why *does* the audience suffer this way? Why does it experience these emotions? It's easy to understand that anyone standing in front of a group of listeners is bound to feel a bit keyed up since he wants to do a good job, but why the audience?

It's very simple. The audience seeks pleasant situations and desperately tries to avoid awkward ones. It finds itself very much tied up with anyone it listens to. It doesn't want to worry, and too many speakers make it do just that!

Put simply, all audiences hate uncertainty. They can't stand the nervous tension of speaker failure. They don't like *hoping* a speaker through his performance. Audiences want to sit back, forget the troubles of the day, and enjoy listening.

But if forced into an unpleasant situation; if forced to listen to a weak speaker who makes them feel uneasy, audiences react quickly. They twist and turn, look at watches, yawn, want to be somewhere else, and most unfortunately, refuse to believe anything the speaker says. As a final step, the audience has a fool-proof escape; they drop a mental Venetian blind with a silent "click" and cut off the speaker competely. Their thoughts are then free to go out to other more pleasant things; drives in the country, golf, vacations, etc. The audience has escaped to instant solitude and peace!

Once this has happened, the speaker has had it! Then he *is* all alone!

This then is your audience. And this is the way you can expect it to act. It wants you to succeed, but won't help

much. It wants to hear a good speech, but doesn't expect
to. It wants to feel at ease, but if it can't, may go to
sleep.

Remember, this is not just the audience you would expect to face in a large auditorium; this is the audience you
meet every day of your life. You face it when you meet
your colleagues on the train in the morning. You meet it
when you speak to a training group in the plant. You meet
it when your boss calls a departmental meeting and wants
you to outline a point of view. You meet it when you stand
up in Town Meeting and point out the need for a new
school.

Your audience is all around you almost all the time, and
if you haven't faced it you are a very rare exception. In
any case, you can be sure of one thing . . . you're going to
have to face it sometime, and you want to be prepared!

Your speech *is* your future! On this point, as Shakespeare said, "There's no hinge or loop to hang a doubt
on."

We've had a long, careful look at your audience: at its
likes and dislikes, its gratifications and its pet peeves. Now
let's see how we can trade on this analysis and win its
approval!

This is not particularly difficult to do if you remember
how the audience feels about the speaker and what it expects him to do. The following suggestions are *musts*.
They all approach the audience from a position of strength
by stressing the positive point of view and clearly stating
your *desire* to take your role as speaker. Apply these guides
and you will give a good speech and win acceptance
from your listeners.

1. You know your audience wants to feel secure. Stand up and talk to them with strength and force. Set them at ease with your positive attitude. Project your voice; be sure you protect against any wavering of tone that might creep in. Let your audience *hear* how secure you are!

2. You know the audience dislikes worrying whether the speaker will succeed or not. Take this worry off their hands. Tell them with definite movement, definite gestures, a decisive manner that you are speaking to them because you want to! Assure them by your physical appearance that you are prepared to handle anything that comes along.

3. You know your audience gets bored easily. Wake them up with vivid language. Startle them with vital imagery—description, dramatic wording, simple but compelling comparisons and contrasts. *You* must keep their attention, they won't give it to you unless you make the effort.

4. You know your audience eats up interesting information. Give it to them. Offer facts, stories, figures, humor, testimony. Vary your interest material, and give them details they can remember easily, because they will be able to understand them easily. Give them facts they can enjoy!

5. Above all, reach out and figuratively shake the hands of your listeners. Tell them you're glad they're there. Tell them they'll profit personally

from what they're about to hear. Most important, tell them that they'll *enjoy* it while it's happening!

Do these things and the audience will be eating out of your hand. Eating facts, that is!

EXERCISES. . . .

1. Imagine greeting a friend of yours who has just returned from a trip. Say the greeting aloud. Now take this same greeting and offer it to an imaginary audience. Instead of saying "Hello, Ted. How was your trip, etc.," Stand up and and say to your audience. For instance, "I understand you've just come back from a trip, etc." Most important of all, make your audience feel the same friendliness you would give to your friend.

2. Pretend you are trying to tell an audience not to worry about your performance. Reassure them with words that they don't have to worry about your feeling nervous, etc. Say the words aloud, and on your feet. Now try to do the same thing without using the direct words. Tell a joke or reassure them about your material. Tell them why they will find the information interesting. Tell them they are all there to have a good time, you will do all the work. Relax them.

3. Just for fun, stand up and tell your imaginary audience about a trip you have taken. Try to stretch it out to three or four minutes. Be animated, try to interest them in the humorous,

exciting details. Now do one more thing. Imagine that they are all smiling, laughing along with you, deeply involved.

These are just some of the practice techniques you can try. They will make your actual performance much, much easier.

Speech Outline for the Direct Talk

Phocion, the Greek, compared the speeches of Leosthenes to cypress trees "They are tall and comely, but bear no fruit."

PLUTARCH

PLUTARCH was pointing out that it is not enough for a speaker simply to feel comfortable in front of his audience. He must have something to say. This is an essential that *every* audience has the right to demand. Content must *not* be an empty word.

The following outline will show you how to prepare and develop an effective speech; a speech that is not only interesting, but valuable to your audience. It stresses brevity and directness; the handmaids of effectiveness.

You may use this outline for all your speeches. It will work equally well for the speech after dinner as for the business speech to convince or persuade. Among its valuable contributions is the way it will guide you from beginning to middle to end in a logical order. This alone will make you a better than average speaker.

Your outline for Direct Talk has 5 steps, each with a

specific purpose. Added together, these five steps form a speech that will gain the audience's continued attention and approval. A speech that moves briskly from opening to close; from idea through development to final suggested conclusion.

Here then is the outline for your next successful speech:

1. COMMAND YOUR AUDIENCE
2. DIRECT YOUR FIRE
3. SAY WHAT YOU MEAN
4. SELL YOUR IDEA
5. GET ACTION

This is the "road map" for your future speaking. Use it in the development of your speech. If you get lost in your delivery, think back to the step where you hesitated. These steps will keep you on the super-highway of good speaking and off those dull and bumpy back roads.

"Themistocles replied that a man's discourse was like to a rich Persian carpet, the beautiful figures and patterns of which can be shown only by spreading and extending it out; when it is contracted and folded up, they are obscure and lost."—PLUTARCH

This outline is designed to spread out your speech carpet; to tell you what to say and in what order. It will help you write your speech; it will help you deliver it. It is perhaps the *most* valuable speaking tool that can be given to you to make you a better speaker. Invest the time to learn the reason and use of each step; each has something important to offer.

Memorize the outline for the Direct Talk . . .

Learn to use it . . .

Practice using it in your next speech . . .

Is it worth it? Ask your audience!

Here again is the outline and the purpose each step serves:

Step 1. *COMMAND YOUR AUDIENCE*

Purpose: —To demand the attention of your listeners.

—To arouse their interest in you and your speech.

—To get the willingness of the audience to listen and perhaps believe what you have to say.

Step 2. *DIRECT YOUR FIRE*

Purpose: —To aim your subject at *this* audience.

—To show *this* audience why *this* subject is important to *them*.

—To demand your listeners' personal involvement in your subject.

Step 3. *SAY WHAT YOU MEAN*

Purpose: —To state clearly the subject or theme of your speech.

—To make absolutely clear *exactly* what you are going to prove, explain, or describe.

—To make it clear just where you stand on the subject to be discussed.

Step 4. *SELL YOUR IDEA*

Purpose: —To expand on your central theme so

that your audience will understand the subject.

—To prove the point you have made to your listeners and make them agree with your position.

—To persuade your audience to abandon their individual beliefs on a subject and join in accepting your way of thinking.

Step 5. *GET ACTION*

Purpose: —To tell your audience what the information you have presented means to them.

—To tell your audience what you want them to do about the subject.

—To get your audience to *ACT!*

These are the guideposts, the ABC's of the good speech. The guideposts that show you how to keep your speech and audience in order.

It is important to remember that your audience has no outline of your speech. In order for your presentation to be successful, they must be able to follow every sentence, every word. If they don't, you may lose them; and you may never get them back. Once that mental Venetian blind falls, it's difficult to raise it again!

This outline will keep your audience with you. It gives them an outline *within* the speech itself. It gives them the simplest, most direct, most logical path through your information. It will answer the questions raised in the minds of your listeners, and it will answer them *as* they arise.

As in all other activities, order is the hardest thing for man to come by. It is, of course, also the most valuable.

In the business speech, there is no substitute for organization.

Command Your Audience

SAMUEL JOHNSON, perhaps the greatest satirist who ever lived, once said of a contemporary, "He is not only dull himself, but the cause of dullness in others."

This is unfortunately the immediate judgment of numberless audiences about endless speakers. Very often this judgment is made right after the speaker has gotten through his *first* sentence! A sentence that has failed completely to command their attention.

If the speaker is to give himself a chance of success, his first contact with his listener must set the pattern; his first contact must stress the positive and lay a solid foundation of security, force and interest. The speaker who is satisfied to wait for the second sentence is "a dollar short and an hour late." His audience won't wait!

The first sentence must be like the salesman's knock on the door—positive . . . direct . . . and attention getting.

Nothing less will do!

> "I should like to address you this evening for the
> next few minutes on some of the primary aspects
> inherent in the fabrication of heavier-than-air
> transport aviation."

What chance do you think an opening remark like this
has to succeed? The answer is simple: NONE! It just won't
do!

Use yourself as a guide. Wouldn't *you* drop the mental
Venetian blind if you were in the audience? What's wrong?
Listen!

> *"I should like to address you . . ."*

(Your audience knows this. That's why you're there!)

> *". . . this evening . . ."*

(They assume it would be this evening.)

> *". . . few minutes . . ."*

(Time, a sore point with generations of audiences. Glad
you brought that up!)

> *". . . primary aspects . . ."*

(About as vague and uninteresting a pair of words as
you could find!)
and on and on and on . . . Violating all the rules of plain
speaking and common sense; avoiding all the ways of
making listeners sit up and take notice. This speaker's
audience will soon be very limited in number during this
performance. As a matter of fact, in this case, the speaker

is *really* alone!

He could have said something like this:

> "There's no mystery in the making of a modern transport plane. Today's jets are still made of that old wonder material . . . 'brains'."

Short. Direct. Attention-getting. A statement like this is *bound* to command the attention and interest of your listeners, and set you off to a flying start.

Let's look closely to see what goes into the making of a good *COMMAND* Step. These are the things you want to do to get your presentation off the ground.

1. Wake up your audience. Take them out of that mental haze.

2. Arouse their interest. Make them lean forward in their seats. Show them that your speech is going to be different; that it is going to be fresh, vital and interesting.

3. Get them to agree to listen favorably to what you have to say. Show them that you not only have facts, but that the facts are easy to listen to.

Will Cuppy, the American humorist, described the Dodo as the only creature he ever knew that was created for the sole purpose of becoming extinct.

The best way for the speaker to become as extinct as the Dodo is to start his speech with a limp, jelly-like opening. Once the audience decides the speaker doesn't have the strength to hold his position of command, they will also decide the whole thing isn't worth the bother. At this point the man "up front" has ceased to be a speaker; he has become a performer!

This leads to the next and obvious question. We know what the *COMMAND* Step is supposed to do, but where can we find the material to do the job? The answer is so close to us all that it's sometimes hard to see!

Draw on the happenings all around you! Look to your experiences, remember your readings, think about the sayings of your friends.

Television is full of material that you can use. Some of the best examples of ideas that can grab and hold an audience are in the advertising that stimulates American business.

One thing is sure. If you look, you can't fail to find an idea vital enough to have your listeners leaning forward in their seats right from the first important sentence!

Here's a list of some of the types of opening remarks that make an effective *COMMAND* Step.

a) A quote from a famous person.
b) An unusual, startling statement.
c) A dramatic story.
d) A reference from the Bible.
e) A reference to a current or well-known news story.
f) A personal experience.
g) A rhetorical question.
h) An historical event.
i) Adventure, past or present.

A list of the possible opening statements you can use for

your *COMMAND* Step would require as much space as can be found in most large libraries. The above list is meant only to trigger your thinking of excellent openings you have stored up in your own mind!

Let's look at some *COMMAND* Steps that do the job they're designed to do . . . to get the favorable attention of your audience from the *first* word!

Remember, the *theme* of your speech will be stated in Step 3. This theme must be clear in your mind before you ever begin to develop your presentation. Then you build a strong *COMMAND* Step and make it tie in.

For example, let's take the following theme for your speech before the Association of National Advertisers: "Advertising Is More Than a Stimulant, It Is a Foundation to Our Entire Economy."

Given this subject, here are some of the ways to *COMMAND YOUR AUDIENCE*. Remember, these are only a few possibilities. There are hundreds of others. Perhaps you already have some in mind. First, a *startling statement*:

> "Let's face it. Talk about American business existing without advertising is like a diver existing without air. In less than six months after advertising was dropped, the entire economy would begin to choke-up and finally suffocate for want of sustenance. How American business would have grown without advertising I do not know. What would happen if advertising was now dropped, I can predict in terrible detail."

You need never doubt that your listeners will now listen to what you have to tell them. This opening will not *allow* them to be disinterested!

Here's another *COMMAND* Step that uses a quotation from the Old Testament to draw the audience into the speech and sets them up to receive the central theme of your presentation. In this case, let's assume that the theme is: "Ten Years From Today, The New Products We Introduce Will Be Returning 75% of Our Profits."

> "3,000 years ago an ancient sage called for the careful guidance of children by parents so that, 'Your children may be as plants grown up in their youth; that your daughters may be as cornerstones.' "

Then you add:

> "We all follow this wise man's advice at home. But do we follow it in our daily business life? Are we raising our 'business children,' our new products, to be the cornerstones of our company?"

This *COMMAND* Step has the basic ingredients necessary for an effective opening statement; interesting information presented dramatically and framed in vivid language.

Now suppose you find yourself asked to speak before the Businessman's Club on the growing problem of Juvenile Delinquency.

The following *COMMAND* Step would call into play the attention-getting qualities of the immediate and vital in the news:

> "*News* . . . Youth Admits Rape Slaying
> *Herald* . . . Boys Stomped to Death for Thrills

> *Times* . . . Juvenile Crime Up 15% in Year
> *Clarion* . . . Torture Teens Admit Killing"

Then you follow it up with,

> "This is *our* city. These are *our* streets; streets *our*
> kids use every day. *We* must take the offensive."

The attention span of an audience has been estimated to be about *eight* seconds. That's approximately the time it takes you to walk four steps! The burden is certainly on the speaker to keep the interest of his audience if he expects to convince them of what he has to say.

A dramatic story is one of the most effective ways to get audience attention. Every one perks up to a well-told, exciting story. Draw one with words that your audience can *see*. Try one like this as a *COMMAND* Step.

> "Picture for a moment a dimly-lighted hall in a
> litter-filled east side tenement. In the deep shadows
> of the stairwell crouches a young boy of about
> ten years. His eyes are filled with a mixture of fear
> and resentment. In his right hand he clutches a
> switch-blade. This boy is bent on murder."

This doesn't have to be an actual situation, but it is a picture your audience will recognize as an accurate description of the conditions in which juvenile delinquency festers and finally explodes into the open. What you have succeeded in doing is to make this situation and the plight of this young boy immediate and alive. And you have done it with words!

There remains one important question about the *COM-*

MAND Step that is still to be answered, "When should it be used?" The answer is another one of those easy ones ... *Always!*

In all types of speeches? Yes! All types! There is no other way to start a speech. You *must* begin with the attention of the listening audience.

Here are some examples of excellent openings to speeches, excellent *COMMAND* Steps by people you probably know.

A rhetorical question is asked by Mr. George E. String-fellow, Senior Vice President, Thomas A. Edison, Inc.

> "What makes America great?" Other nations are as richly endowed with natural resources and their people possess equal ingenuity. Why then has the United States made more progress in 165 years than other nations in 6,000 years? What does America have that other nations do not possess?"

Mr. Theodore R. McKeldin, former Governor of Maryland, speaking at Steed College of Technology, refers to an *historical event:*

> "In Pericles' eulogy to the Athenian dead, which many people regard as the greatest oration ever delivered, the high point was touched when the speaker described Athens as the school of all Greece. More than 2,000 years later we know that Athens was, in fact, more than the school to Greece; to an astonishingly large extent it was the school to the whole world."

Here's an example of an effective use of a *quote* to open

a speech by Mr. Charles E. Wilson, former Secretary of Defense:

> "The great and wise men who founded our nation, early recognized the supreme importance of education in a free society. In 1787 the Congress incorporated the following provision in the Northwest Ordinance: 'Religion, morality, and knowledge being necessary to good government and the happiness of mankind, schools and the means of education shall forever be encouraged.'"

The following is one final example of a vital *COMMAND* Step. In this, Paster Karl H. A. Rest uses the spirit of adventure and everyone's interest in the unknown to demand attention.

> "When the noted archaeologist, Dr. Heinrich Schliemann made his excavations at Mycenae, he discovered a royal tomb which he later identified as the grave of Agamemnon, known by the illustrious title, King of Men. All that remained in the royal tomb was a crown, a shield, a sword, and a few trinkets which had been badly tarnished by age.

> "Where was the head which once so proudly wore the crown, or the strong arm which held the shield, or the quick hand which wielded the sword? Nothing remained but a handful of dust."

Give your audience something interesting that they can listen to and you'll have no problem of gaining their attention and holding it throughout your speech. You'll have your audience sitting forward, wanting to get closer to what you have to say!

A good *COMMAND* Step is a *must* for a good speech. It will spotlight everything that is to follow.

With a rifle it's: *Ready—Aim—Fire*

With your speech it's: *Attention—Interest—Acceptance*

EXERCISES. . . .

1. The theme of your speech is the importance of communications in today's world. Develop the following COMMAND statements:
   a. A quotation from the Bible or history.
   b. A humorous story.
   c. A statement from the newspaper or a news magazine.

The above COMMAND statements can be short indeed. They need not be more than a few sentences. Just be sure they refer directly to the theme of your speech.

2. This is a good time to begin to start your collection of quotes, stories, facts, jokes you will find helpful in future speeches. Get a little black book and start jotting them down. You will find them invaluable.

3. If you can obtain a tape-recorder, record your first efforts on developing a strong, attention-getting COMMAND statement. Play it back. Would it make you sit up and take notice of a speaker?

Direct Your Fire

STEPHEN LEACOCK, the Canadian humorist, wrote of the uncertainty of one of his characters like this: "He flung himself from the room, flung himself upon his horse and rode madly off in all directions."

Leacock was commenting on the confusion and lack of purpose of his mixed-up character. A character who was able to muster plenty of movement, but gain no results; exhibit plenty of action, but with no direction.

Rushing off in all directions is a major sin of many speakers too, and the plague of millions of listeners. A plague the second step of your speech outline is designed to cure.

The *DIRECT YOUR FIRE* Step has one very specific function to perform, one that must be fulfilled in every good speech or presentation—to tell the listener exactly *why* the information he is about to hear is important to him—to tell him exactly why *he* should be listening. This is an all too often forgotten part of most speeches.

Our world is one of intense complexity. Hundreds of objects, ideas, sales messages, colors, forms, motivating forces, etc., are fighting for the attention of your audience every hour of the day. The *DIRECT YOUR FIRE* Step is *your* opportunity to make *your* speech the personal concern of *each* and *every* one of your listeners.

Your job is to pin the importance of your speech idea and theme on everyone present!

Most audiences come uncommitted to listen to a speaker. The attitude is one of "Well, let's see what he's like before we decide to join in or not." Listeners constantly make it very clear that they don't plan to do *any* work at all!

This makes the speaker's job very clear. He must pull the listener into the subject and *make* him be concerned, make him commit himself, make him an active part of the speech situation.

The way to do this is to tell every listener *why* he or she should listen and how the information you have will *directly* effect everyone listening.

Unfortunately, too often speakers fail right here. They hide the reasons that would bring the audience flocking to their side.

It isn't enough for the speaker to state that *he* has seen certain events, that *he* has done certain things, that *he* feels a certain way about a situation. The audience knows these things; they know he has a point of view or he wouldn't be standing before them!

But, the audience always asks, what about us? Where do we come in? How will these ideas touch our lives?

How can this be answered? Like this.

First, for an example, let's go back to your speech on "juvenile delinquency" delivered to the Businessman's Club. Your COMMAND Step went like this:

> "Picture for a moment a dimly-lighted hall in a litter-filled east-side tenement. In the deep shadows of the stairwell crouches a young boy about ten years old. His eyes are filled with a mixture of fear and resentment. In his right hand he clutches a switch blade. This boy is bent on murder!"

Now, your audience needs to be told how this situation directly affects them. They may not live near this slum area. This picture may not be as immediate to them as it is to you. They may even feel that they have enough problems, and that this is just one of those things that exists, unfortunately.

You, as a speaker, must *make* it a personal problem for them. Draw them in. Don't let a single listener feel he doesn't have a stake in this boy.

Try something like this:

> "Over three hundred years ago the English poet John Donne said, 'No man is an island unto himself.' He was pointing out what we all know is *absolutely* true; that the problems of every single individual are our problems and will affect us in some way. If this disgraceful scene of delinquency exists, it is not only the problem of the police, the courts, the welfare organizations. This is our problem; your problem and mine!"

It's difficult for a listener to receive this direct challenge and remain committed. Give him this *DIRECT YOUR FIRE* Step and he'll be *forced* into a position of responsibility.

Let's take another example. Suppose your speech theme to the Planning Board of your company was: "We Should Actively Contribute to a Plan to Improve the Schools in Our Plant Area."

This is hard for anyone to disagree with. None the less, it *is* easy for your listeners to say, "Well, it's certainly too bad in a country of this size that schools should suffer for want of funds. *Someone* should certainly help the schools."

The word "someone" is italicized to make a point. Because school relief is somewhat distant, or perhaps because it's late in the day and people are tired, the listeners are sluffing off your idea. The easy way is to let "someone" handle it. Your proposal is rolling off their backs, and it's not their fault. It's yours!

Remember, school aid is not part of the daily job of your listener. It's naturally difficult for him to feel close to the subject, even a subject he's basically sympathetic to. He's willing to listen, but only as an outsider.

It's the speaker's job to make his listener feel that *he* must be involved to the degree of taking personal action. And this is exactly what the *DIRECT YOUR FIRE* Step is designed to do!

Let's try an approach that goes to the sensitive spots of the listener. An approach like this:

> "I'm not going to ask you to contribute for humanistic reasons alone, for I believe you can all see these clearly. I prefer to ask your support because the

standards of the neighborhood *must* affect our personnel, our efficiency, and finally our product. I believe our contribution to the educational excellence of this area will bring us a realistic and measurable return in dollars and cents."

Here are more examples from actual speeches. Note how the *DIRECT YOUR FIRE* Step pins the importance of the subject to the listening audience.

First, Mr. Ford Q. Elvidge, former Governor of Guam, at the Commencement Day Exercises of the Territorial College of Guam:

> "You should have pride in Guam too. It was only ten years ago this month that this area where we stand and sit this morning was in shambles. Many of you here this morning know more about this than I do—you were *here* then. Many of you saw and heard shells ripping and blasting through the coconut palms, the boondocks and your homes—killing human beings, as the U. S. Marines recaptured the first enemy-held territory in the history of the United States. Much has taken place in those ten years and now a college of education stands where those people fought and died. It should make you proud of your countrymen."

Mr. Elvidge realizes he is telling his audience something they already know. He also knows how important it is to re-vitalize these happenings and direct the theme of his speech to listeners who will be personally involved in his information.

Here's another example. Note how Dr. Carlo Mantilla, member of the Board of Directors and Chairman of the Export Advertising Committee, pinpoints his audience in Detroit:

> "There is hardly a better place in the United States to speak on an economic topic than in your highly industrialized city. And being a Latin American, I can tell you that we—your neighbors to the south —have a high regard and great admiration for your city of Detroit."

In this *DIRECT YOUR FIRE* Step, Mr. Mantilla makes good use of a sincere compliment to touch upon his audience's civic pride and thus draw them all into his speech.

Here's another speaker talking to a group of salesmen. Note how he makes his topic important to the listeners in that room:

> "You know we're building plants. You know we're expanding our territories. You know we have a good product. We know this too. We also know that our product moves because of you, our sales-men. That's why we asked you to come here to New York to let us tell you about our plans for this coming year."

One final example. This speaker is talking to a group of plant supervisors:

> "Last week the president of a large petroleum com-pany spoke to our Board of Trustees. He pointed out several management problems that are peculiar

to our industry. The Board asked me to pass this information directly on to you."

If you assume the members of the audience know why they are there listening to the presentation and don't need to be stimulated, you may assume yourself right out of an audience. You could be right, but not often enough to make it worth the risk. Play safe!

The *DIRECT YOUR FIRE* Step is like the sight on your rifle. It enables you to aim your speech right at the bull's-eye. Don't spray your ammunition in your next speech. Take careful aim; then fire!

EXERCISES. . . .

1. You are speaking to the Woman's Club of your town. You want to urge them to support the construction of a town swimming pool. Some have children, some do not. All know it's going to increase taxes. Develop a Direct Your Fire step that will make this subject each listener's personal problem. Remember the three greatest motivators of the human organism are money, safety and growth in stature. Try an appeal to each of these. See which one you think comes off best.

2. You are suggesting that a major corporation give the space in its lobby to a continuing series of art exhibits. The men you are talking to are serious business men. Their interest in art does not come into their usual business life. Develop a Direct Your Fire step to involve them in your presentation. Perhaps an appeal to their altru-

ism. Perhaps a mention of the great men of the Renaissance who supported art and culture. Do you think you could sufficiently involve them in your speech?

3. You want to get the young men of the town where you live to get interested in politics. They are probably disenchanted with anything political. You think you can convince them they should change their minds. But you must make the subject of interest to them first. You must convince them that your speech is for *them*. How about comparing politics with something they are deeply involved in . . . like football . . . and the team effort. Perhaps you would point out the number of elections won by the young men getting out and campaigning. Can you show them how their future is at stake? That of their young families? Make your Direct Your Fire Step as strong as you can.

Say What You Mean

LISTEN to the good advice of Mr. Clifford Gregg, Director of the Chicago Natural History Museum: "If you have anything to say, I think the best way to express yourself is to say just what you mean."

This simple and straightforward suggestion is as accurate as it is direct. Your author is grateful to Mr. Gregg because the point he is making fits exactly into this book and right into this stage of the outline for Direct Talk. The first steps in your speech outline, the *COMMAND YOUR AUDIENCE* and *DIRECT YOUR FIRE* Steps, are designed to gain attention and to aim your information at your immediate audience. They are carefully planned to bring you, the speaker, to the edge of the water. With Step 3, *SAY WHAT YOU MEAN*, you plunge in. This is the statement of central theme; of your purpose and your position. It is by far the most important single sentence in your entire speech.

Why the *SAY WHAT YOU MEAN* Step, and why at this spot? What does it do? How does it work?

The *SAY WHAT YOU MEAN* Step is a simple statement of exactly *what you are going to talk about*. It is an exact statement of what you plan to prove or develop. It is the center of your entire presentation.

Look at it this way. The *SAY WHAT YOU MEAN* Step is like the center beam of your house. It must be firmly planted, secure, stable, straight. Every other part of the house will add to, build upon this central structure.

The *SAY WHAT YOU MEAN* Step is *vital* to the structure of your speech. All the bits of fact, proof, authority, example, visual aids, etc., that follow will have *one* purpose . . . to support and expand upon this statement. Everything that is said from now on in the speech will refer directly to this step. You must be sure it's stated clearly!

William Wordsworth, the English poet, after listening to Samuel Coleridge speak, commented to a friend that he was carried away by the man's speaking ability. He pointed out Coleridge's style, his flow of words, his excellent gestures. "Of course," he added, "I haven't the faintest idea of what he was talking about."

Unfortunately, his experience is not unique!

Too many listeners leave the room with no more than a foggy idea of the speaker's central theme or his purpose for giving the presentation. The fault lies in his not making the *SAY WHAT YOU MEAN* Step crystal clear!

Remember that one of the major contributions of a speech outline is that it presents information to the listener in a logical order, and at the exact moment that he is asking for it!

In a written report, the central theme can be sharply defined. It may be a paragraph by itself; it may be underlined; it may be in capitals. In some way, it will stand out on the printed page; away from the rest of the material. If the reader has any trouble applying the proof to what the writer is trying to prove, he need only go back and reread that section.

Not so with the listener to a speech. The situation is different; it isn't quite that easy. There is no blueprint for him. The words are not being printed on paper; they are being beamed to him on nothing more substantial than air. The listener must be *absolutely* sure that he knows what the main point of the speech is. Everything that follows will necessarily refer back to it. Not having a printed précis, the listener must be able to follow the speech step by step. How well he can do this depends *completely* on the speaker!

Use the tone and inflection of your voice to underline the *SAY WHAT YOU MEAN* Step. Pause just before you make this statement; say your central theme slowly and clearly, giving it the importance it deserves; pause again after this step, just before going on into your proof. Do everything you can to make this center-point of your speech stand out in block letters a foot high!

The *SAY WHAT YOU MEAN* Step of an oral report to a group of engineers might be like this,

> "The results of our experiments with cold-rolled steel are very favorable. Let me tell you about them."

Incidentally, if you are giving a report, remember that an oral report and a speech are one and the same. A written report and an oral one are completely different breeds. Don't try to speak a report designed to be sent through the mails and read. It's like trying to eat soup with a fork. And the results will be just about as nourishing.

If your report is designed to do more than present information, if it has a definite point of view to offer, be sure that it is included in your *SAY WHAT YOU MEAN* Step. For example:

> "It is not a lack of markets, but the prohibitive cost of building that makes *me* vote against expanding our foreign plants."

This lets your listeners know exactly where you stand. They can start immediately to weigh your reasons for taking this position. This clarity will work all in your favor; audiences are just naturally more favorably disposed to someone who straightforwardly states his stand and simply asks for the opportunity of proving it to his listeners.

Try to phrase your *SAY WHAT YOU MEAN* Step in vivid language your audience *can't* forget. If you can get them to remember your theme, you have that much better chance to get them to believe it! Here's an example from a political speech:

> "Elections are a time for voters to get good government. A vote for Jones will put a political hand in your wallet."

Don't be satisfied with weak, weary, wobbly words. Think of the tremendous advantage you have when a vital phrase strikes home!

A few extra minutes spent on polishing your wording

will pay off handsomely.

Here's an example:

> "The secret of high sales is in the pencils of our engineers."

If we go back to your speech on "Juvenile Delinquency," we'll see how each step serves a specific purpose; points to a definite goal. One Step builds to the next, answering the questions the audience is silently asking, and working together to present a persuasive message.

Watch!

Command your audience
"Picture for a moment a dimly lighted hall in a litter-filled east-side tenement. In the deep shadows of the stairwell crouches a young boy about ten years old. His eyes are filled with a mixture of fear and resentment. In his right hand he clutches a switch blade. This boy is bent on murder!"

Direct your fire
"Over three hundred years ago, the English poet John Donne said, 'No man is an island unto himself'. He was pointing out what we all know is *absolutely* true, that the problems of every single individual are *our* problems and will affect us all in some way. If this disgrace exists, it is not only the problem of the police, the courts, the welfare organizations. It is *our* problem; yours and mine!"

Say   "I have a plan I want you to consider; a
what   plan which will not reduce juvenile de-
you mean   linquency in our city—it will *wipe it out*."

Your speech has marched along briskly with a vitality
which will constantly stimulate and reward your listeners.
You are leading and your audience will follow. You are
speaking effectively!

Here are a few additional reminders about using the *SAY
WHAT YOU MEAN* Step:

1. Don't assume your audience automatically
   knows what your central theme is . . . tell them!

2. Don't present your *SAY WHAT YOU MEAN*
   Step in question form. It confuses the audience.

3. Don't mix this step with any other. It can only
   weaken your speech.

4. Be careful your audience doesn't confuse the
   SAY WHAT YOU MEAN Step with the proof
   that will follow it. Show by your voice that
   this is your central idea.

5. If you have *any* doubt about the clarity of your
   presentation of this step—stop! Don't go any
   further until you're *sure* it's completely clear!

Up to this point you have been preparing your listeners
for the core of your speech; the idea you want to get across.

Now they know exactly *what* you want to talk about.
From now on your goal is crystal clear. Now you must
prove it!

EXERCISES. . . .

You have now reviewed the first three steps of the Outline for Direct talk. We have looked at the Command Your Audience step, the Direct Your Fire step, and the Say What You Mean step. Each step does a special job. Each is *essential* to *every* good speech. Now do the following exercises for practice.

The following are themes of speeches. They are the Say What You Mean steps of presentations. For practice, take each theme and build a Command step and a Direct Your Fire step. Be sure you get audience attention; be sure you make the theme of importance to the audience you are speaking to. Here are the themes.

1. You are a salesman speaking to a meeting of salesmen. "Extra sales don't come from making more calls, they come from knowing what your customers want."

2. You are talking to a special meeting of the School Board.
   "The Fairchild School should drop inter-school football. It does not teach sportsmanship, it teaches violence."

3. You are addressing a meeting of a Woman's Liberation group. Your theme is . . .
   "Wherever women have entered the politics of world affairs, they have done far, far better than men in maintaining the peace."

4. You are speaking to a group of businessmen. Your subject is . . .
   "The pattern of business organizations to delegate authority down to the lower levels is pass-

ing out of existence. Today's business is being
run at as high a level of the company as possible."

In each of the above situations develop a strong Command
Your Audience step and an equally demanding Direct
Your Fire step. When you've finished, stand up and deliver
them aloud. As you would to your audience.

Sell Your Idea

*"There is no adequate defense, except stupidity,
against the impact of a new idea."*

PERCY W. BRIDGMAN

ALL TALK, conversation, discussion, debate, argument, chat, harangue is made up of a statement of the speaker's position and proof to back up that statement. Throughout the day you are following the age-old pattern of statement . . . proof.

Perhaps it goes something like this:

JIM: "Let's go to the ball game tonight."
ANDY: "I'd rather go to the movies."
JIM: "You don't want to go to the movies."

Proof . . . "Just think how nice it will be to sit out in the open; how cool it will be."

Proof . . . "The game should be good too. New York is in first place, you know!"

Everyone is willing to listen to almost any point of view on a subject. At the same time, almost everyone will demand "reasons why" before he will accept another point of view as his own.

Facts are the general name given to those materials used to back up and prove statements of personal point of view. They encompass illustrations, examples, analogies, testimony, logic, statistics, figures, visuals, etc.; all important devices which serve the speaker in presenting ideas which prove to the listener that what the speaker has said is reasonable, acceptable and right.

The *SELL YOUR IDEA* Step is always the step that separates the good speakers from the poor ones. The quality and presentation of facts have always, throughout the history of man, determined the direction the listeners have taken and the speed with which ideas and institutions have changed. It is here that the value of facts framed in the spoken word have shown their tremendous strength.

Bernard Baruch has defined the importance of facts like this: "Everyone has the right to be wrong in his opinion, but no one has the right to be wrong in his facts."

The strength of the facts in the *SELL YOUR IDEA* Step will, more than *any other* single step in the Outline for Direct Talk, make you the speaker your listeners want to hear; the speaker they want to believe; the speaker whose advice and suggestions they will follow.

Your choice of facts *must* be determined by your speech and specifically by what you want to prove. Your choice of *how* you will *SELL YOUR IDEA* demands a full understanding of the types of proof available to you.

The next several pages will discuss the different types of proof and present examples of their use in speeches by businessmen, educators, politicians, clergymen; all speakers who have learned by experience how to use the rarest of all material—*Facts.*

SELL YOUR IDEA . . . WITH EXAMPLES

The single, all important purpose of the artist is to make people "see."

The speaker also has this as his overriding goal. He must make people *see* and then make them *accept* and finally make them *act.*

Perhaps the most effective method of making your idea clear to your audience is to "show" them; to give them examples to make them understand the point you have presented. Examples make ideas live more vividly; help your listeners understand your thought by seeing the idea in action; help your listeners accept your idea by showing them that what you are speaking of has happened before in a similar way.

For instance, Mr. John Jay Hopkins, formerly President of General Dynamics Corporation, uses this example to *SELL HIS IDEA* on the peaceful use of atomic materials:

> "For example, through the use of radio-phorous—which checks the overproduction of red blood cells in the bone marrow—lives of sufferers from leukemia have been prolonged. . . . The second largest application [of isotopic materials] is in the field of medicine."

It is never enough for the speaker to simply state his idea and expect it to be accepted. To gain the understanding of the listener, the speaker *must* make that idea recognizable to the audience. One of the most effective ways is through the use of examples.

In the following speech delivered to a group of salesmen, Harold Drown, D.D., makes the point that confidence and effort pay off. Note the use of examples:

> "Think on this, you salesmen who are timid about going forward against opposition. One time the majority said, 'The world is flat, and death lies at its edge.'
>
> Columbus said 'No, it isn't and I'll prove it.' And because of him, you and I live in a magnificent land. Once the majority said, 'You can't drive a boat with steam.' Fulton said, 'Yes you can. And I'll prove it.' And civilization took a tremendous leap upwards."

Examples stand up behind the speaker's ideas and tell the audience, "You see, what the speaker says is right. It's happening all the time."

Let's look at one more example to illustrate how they can be used by the speaker to *SELL HIS IDEA*. Here Mr. Fred Lazarus, Jr., uses an example to support his idea that department store selling techniques must be improved:

> "In May, 1954, a large metropolitan newspaper in an important industrial area carried a story of a check on selling services. Twenty-seven people had been given ten dollars each with instructions to spend it all quickly—within half an hour. The frustrated shoppers returned at the end of the specified period with the report that they could spend only $56.80 of the $270, because clerks couldn't or wouldn't wait on them. Not one of the shoppers had been able to spend his full $10 and

abide by the rules. Many of them reported a tremendous indifference on the part of the clerks. Many of them completely ignored the customers."

It is difficult for audiences to stand up to examples like the above without being swayed to the speaker's way of thinking. And that is what a speech is for; to make the listener accept the speaker's information and finally, to do what he asks.

Use examples in your next effective speech!

SELL YOUR IDEA . . . WITH STORIES

"Tell me a story" is probably one of the oldest requests of mankind. It is safe to say that nothing intrigues the human being, from crawling baby to creaking old man as much as a good tale. Audiences, with all their quirks are no different. They *love* stories, particularly they love funny ones!

Every good speaker should have a basketful of point-proving stories that can be pulled out and used to make his audience open up and buy his idea with gusto!

Since you have gone on the line stating that you want to be a *good* speaker, one your audiences will clamor to listen to again, you must learn to use stories and particularly humorous ones.

You hear reams of talk about how difficult it is to tell a good story, about the fact that you can't define humor, about how cold audiences are and how they take on the "O.K., make me laugh" attitude when the speaker steps up to *SELL HIS IDEA* with a humorous story. True? *Bosh!*

Here are some more realistic facts:

Audiences *love* anything that can lighten the air in the speech situation!

We know humor can't be defined accurately. O.K., neither can many other things we live very close to . . . love, hate, etc. The fact still remains that humor is part of everyone of us, and we all desire it!

Anybody, yes, anybody can tell a good story. If you can't do it as well as some other people you know, you can do it well enough to make story-telling a vital part of your speech arsenal. If someone else tells stories better, it's probably because he's had more practice . . . and because he's tried and tried until he's finally succeeded!

When everything else has failed to win the agreement of the audience, the good story will! In fact the story, many times, seems to be the *only* technique that will allow a listener to drop his prejudices and turn around on his own opinion and agree *with* you, the speaker.

William Shakespeare said, "If to do were as easy as to know, paupers' cottages would be princes' palaces." No one can ever deny that it takes practice to do anything well, and story-telling is no exception. But you will gain an all-powerful speaking tool if you exert yourself!

Use these guideposts:

——Tell stories you *know*. One sure way to get mixed up is to try to tell one you're not sure of. The after-dinner speaker has, unfortunately, often been described as "A man who eats a dinner he doesn't want, tells stories he doesn't know, to people who have heard them already."

——Avoid telling stories that depend on a "punch line" to put them over unless you are *sure* it is a good story that the audience will understand easily. You'll be safer telling easy-going stories that tickle the listener with their warm, natural humor.

——Whatever story you tell, it *must* tie in with your speech. If the story doesn't support your point, drop it like a hot potato!

——Make your stories short. Audiences set rules for humor as for anything else in the speech . . . they want to get to the point quickly and move on!

——Beware of the old, old, old stories *everyone* has heard before! If you're not sure of a story, ask a good friend who will tell you if this is worth the telling. Nothing is more deadly than that "Oh here comes that old one again" audience response.

——*Never, never, never* lead into a story with that pet peeve of every audience, "That reminds me of a story . . ." Most listeners leave a speaker right here! This is a red flag that says to the audience that this fellow is long-winded, he thinks he's a funny man, plans to try out old jokes, etc. *Don't!*

——If you *must* tell off-color stories, be prepared to do so at your peril. Male listeners who bellow at a joke when alone, very often sit quiet as mice when the same story is told in public. Be careful! You're on dangerous ground.

——Don't wait for, or show you expect, any response to your story. Just go right on with your speech. If your audience wants to laugh or applaud, stop and let them enjoy themselves. Moral—let *them* make the first move. Use Bob Hope for a model . . . notice he never waits for a laugh, but stops when the laughter comes.

——Keep a book of good stories you have heard or read. You can always go back and use them when you have to build a good speech.

Stories and humor are solid weapons to break down resistance in an audience. You owe it to yourself to learn to use them! Some speech situations, like the after-dinner speech, shouldn't be made without humor.

Audiences may forget facts, statistics, reasons, etc.; but they never forget a good story or the teller. Use humor in your next speech; make your audience remember you!

SELL YOUR IDEA . . . WITH COMPARISONS AND CONTRASTS

Comparisons and contrasts are simply another way of making information clearer to your listener by placing it side by side with another happening and letting him look at both. They are an excellent answer to the listener who asks, and rightfully so, "Show me."

For instance, an airline wants to show that it can carry freight at a low rate, so it compares the cost of carrying a ton of material to Buffalo with its major competitors, the truckers and the railroad.

For instance, a speaker wants to point out that Russia is paying more attention to her education system than we are by raising the wages of teachers. To make this clear, the speaker shows that in the U. S. a teacher makes about 1½ times as much as a laborer; in Russia the teacher makes 8½ times as much.

Comparison and contrast *SELLS YOUR IDEA* by setting your idea side by side with others and letting the audience *see* why your idea is right!

Here are comparisons and contrasts used by speakers who use them well.

Gardner Cowles, former Chairman of the Board of *Look* magazine, speaks of a past trip to Russia:

> "It is curious to me that the countries nearest Russia seem to fear her least while we, the country farthest away, seem to fear her most. The Turks, for example, have fought Russia some 77 times in the last 900 years; yet Turkish experts tell me the Turkish Army would welcome war with Russia and have no doubt about the outcome."

Mr. William McGrath, Cincinnati industrialist speaking on America's ability to produce contrasts the old with the new:

> "We have learned that there is no limit to human desires, and that upon them can be built a limitless volume of production, jobs, and payrolls.
> "This did not happen overnight. Originally, the United States was an underdeveloped country. Less than 100 years ago a large share of our people still lived in one-room log cabins."

Ex-President Herbert Hoover speaks on the value of the Boys' Club organization in the physical development of the youth of the country:

> "As to the physical benefit to the boys, I might
> mention that the national rate of 4-F's was over
> 30% in the last war. A canvass of 200,000 alumni
> of Boys' Clubs showed only 4½%. And they fought
> and died bravely."

The use of comparisons and contrasts is an excellent way
to pull out and exhibit the full value and importance of a
fact you want to use to support your speech.

SELL YOUR IDEA ... WITH ANALOGIES AND SIMILES

Analogies and similes are part of the vital, effervescent
efforts of the human being to add color and sparkle to his
way of saying things. They demonstrate living proof that
everything can be worded in a way to make it more interesting; to make it stick more firmly in the listener's mind!

By definition, similes and analogies are simple comparisons of things that are not alike, but which have one aspect
in common.

Here are some examples. The first is by John Badeau when
President of the Near East Foundation:

> "What should the West do to cement its relations
> with the Middle East? The difficulty with answer-
> ing this question easily is that you can't unscramble
> eggs, and a great many of the Eastern attitudes
> toward the United States are the results of the eggs
> that were scrambled in the past."

In this example, Dr. Henry Baker, formerly Professor of

Marketing at the University of Utah defines "Selling" in new, fresh terms: "Selling, the Greatest Show On Earth in Business and Industry."

You can bet the audience listening to SeaBee Tex Gardiner describe life in the Antarctic came away with these following similes echoing in their minds:

> "Living in the Antarctic is like sitting in a refrigerator with the light on."

> "What really scared you was riding up to the lip of a crevasse and hanging there in a bulldozer, weighing 37 tons. It was like driving a heavy vehicle across the glass roof of Penn Station."

One final famous simile by the great English critic, Dr. Samuel Johnson, who replied when told there was a woman preacher in Scotland:

> "A woman preacher is like a dog walking on its hind legs. It is not done well, but one is surprised to see it done at all."

The use of analogies and similes tend to separate the men from the boys in speaking! The good speaker will take a few minutes more time in the preparation of his speech to come up with a vitally worded comparison that will strike sparks for his listeners. The phrase that sticks will make an audience recall, "Remember that fellow who compared . . . etc., in that sales meeting in New York." They will remember you *and* your sales theme.

SELL YOUR IDEAS with analogies and similes for a speech that sparks!

SELL YOUR IDEA ... WITH NUMBERS

The use of numbers is certainly one of man's earliest building blocks in his development and storing of knowledge. One of his most important communicating symbols. Psychologists tell us that other animals recognize numbers, but only man *uses* them to reason with and to pass ideas and to prove concepts.

Now let's take a moment to see what numbers really are and then how they can best be used by the speaker to reason with the audience and to *SELL HIS IDEAS*.

Numbers are *symbols* which have been developed by man to communicate ideas of quantity, size and shape. These symbols must be *translated* by the reader, (by the listener in the speech situation) and applied in order for him to understand the object or concept being described.

It is the job of the speaker to see that this translation is made as easy as possible!

Look at it this way. If the speaker says, "The vertiginous exegesis precipitated somnolent lethargy," he will have considerably less of an audience than if he said, "The fuzzy comments put them to sleep."

In the first case, the speaker is expecting the audience to do the impossible in translating his words. In the second, the speaker has made the translation easy *by using words that are part of the everyday world of each of us!*

The same must be done in the presentation of numbers and statistics!

Here are some suggestions pointing out how this can be done:

1. Don't use *too many* numbers; don't let the numbers take over in your speech and become more important than the point you are trying to prove. Never forget the numbers are *support* to your speech.

2. Translate your numbers and statistics for your audience. Break them down by comparing them with units that are a part of your listeners' everyday living. For instance, "That's enough fuel for you to run your oil burner for 25 years."

3. Avoid wasting your listeners' time while you build up *long* tables of numbers; focus your attention (and the audience's) on the *point* your numbers make.

4. Don't be finicky with numbers or statistics. Round them off wherever possible, particularly when the numbers are large. Too much precision seems like fussiness to the listener!

5. Remember, the source of your statistics will help *SELL YOUR IDEA*. Audiences have learned to suspect that figures can be twisted to suit the speaker. Make *good* sources support you!

6. Look for unusual figures to stimulate and excite your listeners. Audiences respond to unusual numbers in the same way they respond to unusual happenings. Always look for the dramatic and vital to capture the imagination of your listeners!

Here are some examples of the use of numbers that add

strength and vitality to the speaker's presentation:

> "NATO now has 4 battalions of Corporal missiles. These 4 battalions are equal in fire power to *all* the artillery used in World War II on *all* fronts."

Here Eddy Gilmore, former Associated Press chief in Moscow compares prices in Russia and the U. S. Note how he makes the numbers "live."

> "The Russians have had 6 price reductions since the end of the War, and the last one, under the government of Georgi Malenkov, was a really good one— it reduced items 50%. But after the 6th price reduction, (and that was just before I left Moscow) some of the prices were: One egg, 20 cents; one orange, 55 cents; one pound of steak, $8.20; one pair of ladies' shoes, $36. I say that was after the 6th price reduction."

Professor Leslie G. Moeller, Director of the Iowa School of Journalism hammers home his theme that the youth of America can learn from newspapers and news magazines and that parents must see that these media are supported:

> "Take the case of the most widely circulated news magazine, *Time*. Its 2,627,000 circulation is impressive and growing, but reaches about only one U. S. home in 19. *Newsweek* reaches about one in 33, and *United States News* about one in 49. Or consider the case of the *Atlantic Monthly*, one of the really great magazines of opinion and information; in a nation of almost 160,000,000 persons, the

Atlantic has only 272,600 subscribers, and there is one chance in 319 that Johnny's parents are subscribers to it."

And Professor Moeller concludes:

"Let us assume that Mr. and Mrs. Johnny are willing to find an additional $3 a year (perhaps this comes through missing every 50th cigarette, or in some comparable fashion) for the improvement of their service from the press."

And one final example of the dramatic use of statistics:

"In 1850, only about one-fortieth of the population consisted of individuals older than 65; in 1953 nearly one-tenth of our population were in this age group. In 1955, there were living in the United States 14.3 million people over 65. Of these more than 4,000 were 100 years old or older."

Numbers and statistics can provide solid and forceful proof for your speeches. Use them carefully and selectively; phrase them vitally and vividly. Make them live!

SELL YOUR IDEA . . . WITH AUTHORITY . . . TESTIMONY . . . QUOTES

> *"My left is broken, my right is weakened; the situation is excellent. I am attacking!"*
> MARSHALL FOCH (at the Marne)

In one sense, the speaker need never be *alone* on the platform. He always has strong friends he can call upon to back up the point he is presenting to the audience. These friends are called authority, testimony and quotes.

Very often your audience will refuse to accept an idea with only your *own* authority behind it. Perhaps it's a point that they feel strongly about . . . in a way opposite to your point of view. Perhaps it's because they feel the subject demands more authority than the speaker can give it. Perhaps all they are looking for is a bit more convincing. Whatever the reason, the speaker has to reach into his bag of proof and come up with something that will help him *SELL HIS IDEA*. The way is easy to find if you know where to look!

The use of authority, testimony or quotes is simply the mustering of intelligent support for your position from people living and dead who have gone on record as agreeing with you.

What the speaker is doing when he uses this type of support is to say to the audience,

> "Now some of you seem to need more persuading that what I have been telling you is right. You seem to want more proof. Well, that proof is easy to find. I'm not the only one who has presented this idea, . . . I'm going to let George Washington and Thomas Jefferson tell you how *they* feel about this subject."

Suppose you were going out after a new job and you needed references. Could you find better ones than Washington or Jefferson? What better endorsement could you get than Einstein or Baruch?

This is just the effect the quoting of such authority will have upon your listeners. They will recognize the stature and intelligence of the people standing behind your point of view, and they will find they have to agree with what you say.

Authority and quotes are powerful forces for the speaker, *if* he uses them correctly!

Here are some guides for the use of this type support:

1. Be sure your authority is recognized as someone who has the right to speak on the subject; someone who knows the subject firsthand.

2. Choose an authority who will be accepted by your listener as someone who is free of prejudice; someone the listener will not reject as having an ax to grind.

3. Recognize the difference in audience appeal between authoritative testimony by an expert and quotation from a book or by a historical figure. Testimony will usually support the speaker's point most effectively on questions of *fact*; quotation will usually work much more strongly to get an *emotional* acceptance from the audience.

4. Stay away from hackneyed quotations whose triteness can only have a sickening effect on your audience, i.e., "Well, East is East and West is West, and if they can't meet, how can we?"

5. Don't stretch a quotation all out of shape to make it fit into your speech. A quote like this: " 'I think that I shall never see, a poem lovely as

a tree,' but remember when you are landscaping your house, you need bushes too."

Unfortunately, you hear this kind of absurdity all *too* often, and the audience never fails to wince!

Note this use of authority by Mr. Earl Ubell, Science Editor for a major TV network, in his discussion of the atom:

> "Dr. James Rainwater, professor of physics, said that measurements indicate that the core of the atom is probably like a flattened peach—fluffy on the outside, dense on the inside."

George E. Stringfellow, calls up Abe Lincoln to affirm the theme of his speech, that liberty is held by the determined action of *all* the people.

> " 'To sin by silence,' said Abraham Lincoln, 'when they should protest, makes cowards of men.' Our liberties were not won by cowards and I assure you they will not be preserved by such characters."

In the following example of authority, Robert E. Wilson, former Chairman of the Board of the Standard Oil Company of Indiana, gets solid support from John McCaffery, former chief executive officer of International Harvester, for his speech theme that the universities must supply executives for business and industry, and that business must therefore help support the universities financially:

> "As Mr. McCaffery has said, the chief executive of a company has no great problem in finding men to

run a section or a department, where one line of work is followed. But he loses a lot of sleep over the problem of finding executives who have wider knowledge, more general savvy, and enough background of the right kind to run a whole group of things."

Audiences never fail to respond to quotes by famous men; from literature; from the Bible; sayings that the speaker can use as supports for the idea he wants to drive home. For instance, if you are speaking on the need for executives to think out a problem carefully before they act, you might use this quote from Plutarch:

"I do not think him a good shoemaker who makes a great shoe for a small foot."

Or, if you are speaking on the need for better spoken communication in business today, you might quote Daniel Webster, the great orator:

"If all my possessions were taken from me with one exception, I would choose to keep the power of speech, for with it I would soon regain all the rest."

Perhaps the central theme of your speech is for greater dedication to the job and a stronger holding to beliefs. You could quote Abraham Davenport, advisor to George Washington, to whom the suggestion of a meeting adjournment was made because of the approach of the British. He answered:

"The Day of Judgment is either approaching or it is not. If it is not, there is no cause for adjournment.

If it is, I choose to be found doing my duty. I wish, therefore, that candles may be brought."

And here's a quote that could hammer home your theme that deals with the Russians are a ticklish affair:

"He who eats with the Devil had better use a long spoon!"

The use of quotations trade heavily on several powerful forces of motivation; the strength of the source, the pertinence of the statement to today's situation, and the emotional impact which seems to encircle the glorious past. All these are subtle and effective pressures which move your audience to accept what you have to say, and help you *SELL YOUR IDEA*.

Above the main entrance of the United Nations in New York City is the *theme* of that great organization emblazoned in the following quote:

"They shall beat their swords into plowshares, and their spears into pruning hooks; nations shall not lift up sword against nation, neither shall they learn war anymore."

SELL YOUR IDEA ... With Logical Reasoning

A Roman divorced from his wife, being highly blamed by his friends, who demanded, "Was she not chaste? Was she not fair? Was she not fruitful?" holding out his shoe, asked them whether it was not new and well made. "Yet," added he, "none of you can tell me where it pinches me."

PLUTARCH

"Well, go back and reason with him" is a phrase very common to our everyday life. It is a positive and helpful phrase since it underlines the faith most people have in the power of reason in persuading people to act the way you wish whether it's to build a new school or change a vacation schedule.

Logic is a technical sounding word which has become more formidable by its extensive use in philosophy. For the speaker, however, it need only mean "a reasonable explanation of *why* something should be done the way the speaker suggests."

Let's look at it this way. Logical reasoning uses all the ways of *SELLING YOUR IDEA* we have so far presented and it adds one additional important factor—an order which makes the idea most acceptable.

The need for logical reasoning in the speech is clear; proof alone is not enough, the speech must move reasonably from beginning to end; it *must* track!

Very simply, the reasoning you will use in your speeches is of two kinds:

1. From a listing of causes to the results of these causes, or,
2. From the results back to the original causes.

For example, let's assume you have the task of reporting on the sales decline of your company's new liquid detergent, Splash, in the Baltimore district. If your pattern of presentation was from cause to effect, it would go like this:

a) "Three weeks before we entered the Baltimore market, Lanson & Bros. hit us with a price pack which had the effect of loading the consumer."

In addition:

b) "On our first field trip we found that we had
   not been successful in getting the shelf space
   we normally can expect with a new product."

Plus this:

c) "Recent research points out strongly that
   women don't like the clear color of Splash.
   They seem to want to see the color of the detergent in their dish water."

Perhaps most important:

d) "Because of the softness of the water in this
   area, we were never able to get the share of
   market we expected to take away from the
   package soap products."

Therefore . . . (conclusion):

"Our market share has seriously declined from 3.2
in March to only 1.4 today."

This is reasoning from causes to final effect. Now let's
see how the same material would be presented if reasoning
from effect to causes . . . from conclusion to "reason why."

"Our market share has seriously declined from 3.2
in March to only 1.4 today."
"Why? I think we know the reasons."

a) "Three weeks before we entered the Baltimore
   market, Lanson & Bros. hit us with a price pack
   that had the effect of loading the consumer."

In addition:

b) "On our first field trip we found that we had not been successful in getting the shelf space we normally can expect with a new product."

Plus this:

c) "Recent research points out, etc . . ."

You should realize that you use both these patterns of logical reasoning every day. Carry them over to your speaking and see how they lead your listeners to your point of view.

These patterns of logic are important enough to take a look at another example. Let's assume you have been elected to the Businessmen's Council for a new school. Your presentation might go like this. First, from causes to result.

a) The population of this town has increased 42% in the last two years.

b) The number of children ready for high school next year will be 28% greater than this year . . . approximately 550 new students entering an already overcrowded school.

c) Since we do not have a new school, real estate values are falling. People will move out of the town to find areas with better education facilities. As a result town income will fall.

d) Because of the lack of a good high school, other towns and cities are luring good teachers away.

e) The same thing happened ten years ago in

Roxfort, and they haven't been able to correct it to this day, etc.

Therefore . . . (conclusion):

Our children are poorly educated, in poor facilities, for poor reasons . . . in a wealthy town! We *must* have a new high school!

Now let's use method number two, from the results *back* to the causes:

We have heard members of the town meeting stand before us and tell us we need a new high school; that our children are poorly educated, in poor schools, for poor reasons. Let's go back and see why this is an important step for the town to take.

a) The population of the town has increased 42% in the last two years.

b) The number of children ready for high school next year will be 28% greater than this year . . . approximately 550 new students, etc.

c) If the new school is not built, real estate values will fall, etc.

d) Because of the lack of a good high school, teachers are being lured away, etc.

e) The same thing happened in Roxfort, etc.

To review, there are two basic reasoning patterns you can follow in presenting your point to an audience; patterns that will appeal to the listener's desire for a speech that develops logically and is therefore easy to listen to.

First, you can *review the causes* and tell them what the result is or will be. Second, you can *tell them what has happened*, and then tell them what the causes are.

One final thought; keep your reasoning direct and to the point. Keep in mind Ralph Waldo Emerson's simple and invaluable advice, "Nothing astonishes men so much as common sense and plain dealing."

EXERCISES. . . .

The quality of the proof you use to Sell Your Idea will determine whether your audience believes you or not. When people believe you, they look up to you. If you want to grow in business or in the world around you, you must *work* at it. Doing the following exercises are a step in the right direction. .

1. Collect five examples of proof using examples. (Look in newspapers, magazines, listen to speeches.)

2. Write down five stories you might use sometime to Sell Your Idea. (Listen to friends, TV, anthologies of humor, joke books.)

3. Collect five similes for use in some speech you might give in the future. ("The thinking of some people is about as firm as a wet muffin," etc.)

4. Take the following numbers and dramatize them, i.e. "The latest Japanese tanker is 800 yards long. They could play eight football games simultaneously end to end on her deck."

   a. 250,000 miles of paper.

   b. 170 degrees of heat.

    c. 100 selling calls. (Perhaps you estimate the number of words spoken and compare to the number of words in a book.)

    d. 700 million people.

5. Collect ten quotes from the Bible, history, etc. Save them in a book. You'll need them in the future.

Use Visuals To Prove Your Point

"Give me the ocular proof!"

WILLIAM SHAKESPEARE

IN 1869, a Spanish nobleman named Don Marcelino de Sautuola was out hunting and came upon a large crack in a rock that led downward into a huge echoing cave. As the Spanish lord's eyes became accustomed to the dim light, he suddenly realized he was surrounded by terrifying figures of threatening men and beasts. As the nobleman's eyes searched the darkness, he began to realize the true value of his find. The pictures he was staring at were drawn in the dim ages when man was just beginning to emerge from the dark recesses of the caves and to look out blinking over the rolling hills of the earth. These pictures had been drawn by early men 50,000 years in the past. Fifty millenniums ago fur-clad men stood in the flickering light of oil lamps to draw pictures; pictures which would *show* other watchers what they wanted to say! The picture was being used to present an idea vividly.

It's a long step from the prehistoric cave-dwellers to today's speaker, but the rule that the best way to get across a point is with a picture still remains unchanged.

And no better way will *ever* be found! The picture communicates an idea quicker, clearer and more vividly than any other means of communication! The picture on the cave wall, the visual presentation in the speech—both stick the idea *deep* in the listener's mind. And *that*, after all, is right on target!

Let's take a closer look at this "picture presentation" of ideas; this technique called visual aids. How do they work on the viewer? What purpose do they fulfill in the straightforward selling of an idea? These are two questions that can be answered easily. There is no deep secret in supporting your speech with visuals; no mystery about what the visual can do for you and your ideas.

Here's a definition for your book; a definition which you can use as a check every time you want to use a visual support in your speech.

A visual aid in a speech is a pictorial presentation of an idea or situation used by the speaker because *it looks more like the idea than words or numbers can.*

For instance, a picture or diagram showing how to butcher a side of beef looks more like the actual operation than words that say, "Now take the beef and cut off a brisket, etc."

Or, a pictograph or line graph showing the growth of Russian troop concentrations in East Berlin will certainly show that growth more clearly and vividly than any series of numbers ever could.

The reason for a visual aid is simply to present an idea in

a form that the audience will understand most quickly; in a form which is as close to the real thing as possible; in a form which asks the listener to do as little translating as possible.

Put into a formula it could read like this:

$$\text{The Speaker's Ideas} + \text{Visual Aids}$$
$$= \text{Quick Registration of Idea}$$

Just as in golf, gardening, cooking or cartography, you need a working knowledge or basic rules to use visuals well. In golf the decision is, "What club?" In gardening, "How deep do I plant?" In cooking, "When do I add the condiment?" In cartography, "What type of map shall I make?"

There are beginning rules in each of these activities that answer these questions. There are likewise basic guides to help the speaker learn to make better use of visual aids.

Review these suggestions next time you decide to support your idea visually. They will make and *not* break your visual presentation!

LIGHTS

The speaker must *never* be in the dark! Not even when slides and films are being shown? *Never!* The visual presentation supports what the *speaker* is attempting to develop or prove. He must always be *the* most important object in the room. The visual must always work *for* him! It is impossible for him to assume any importance if the audience can't see him!

If the type of visual presentation demands complete darkness, arrange to have a small light on yourself. If you

don't, you can be sure your authority will be weakened
. . . a serious mistake!

SIZE

The author would like to make a personal plea here. A
plea that the following statement be dropped forever from
all speeches to the end of time!

"I have here a chart of the plant (*pause*) . . . you probably can't see it (*pause*) . . . but I thought it might help
you understand the problem."

Idiotic! How could a chart no one can see help *anyone*
understand the problem? A visual your audience can't see
is *not* a visual aid, and the speaker is wasting his time and
his audience's using it as such!

How can you tell that everyone will be able to see a
visual? Easy! Go to the back of the hall before the speech
and look! If you can see *everything* on the visual, it ful-
fills the requirements.

HOW TO STAND

The right-handed speaker usually stands to the left of
the visual and directs the attention of the audience to his
material. If you use a pointer, you may stand on either side
of the visual, wherever you feel most comfortable. *Don't*,
however, stand in front of the diagram or picture you want
your audience to see. Think about this before you set up
your material; place your diagram where it will be most
visible and where you work easily. Always remember the
importance of integrating the visual to support what you
have to say. If you appear awkward, or the visual is cum-
bersome, its effectiveness in getting to your listeners will

be greatly reduced.

Many speakers fail to use their good visuals fully. Always pull the eye of the viewer down to your chart or visual; point out specifically with your pointer what you want him to note carefully. *Don't* simply wave in the general direction of the visual and expect the viewer to pinpoint the thought!

HOW TO SPEAK

Remember, your audience is the listener, not that inanimate object, the visual. Yet, in nine of ten speeches you listen to, the speaker will spend *most* of his time addressing the visual aid! Speak to the audience! When you turn to the visual, do so to draw the audience's attention down to a particular point that the diagram amplifies or makes more clear. The visual is a help; never let it take *you* from your listeners!

HOW TO USE COLOR

Percy Bysshe Shelley, one of the great poets of the English language, referred to life as "a dome of many-colored glass." He was vividly describing the multicolored, varied nature of our everyday existence, and the effect that color has upon all of us. Look at a picture, an ad in a magazine, a photograph taken by a friend on a vacation, a new car; all are more exciting by their use of color. Color plays an important role everyday in motivating us to accept, and sometimes to reject ideas. However, the important fact is that it forces us to respond. The speaker is losing out if he does not take advantage of this vital force.

HOW TO DRAW

Ever looked at a Japanese print? It's delicate and fine-lined, suggests softness and fragility. These are not the qualities the speaker wants to get across to his fact-hungry and critical audience. He wants to impress his listeners with the strength of his thinking. Strong diagrams and charts can help put this feeling across!

Make the pictures and lines of your visuals *definite, broad* and *clear*. Avoid thinness and delicacy; it can easily be confused with artiness, willingness to compromise and unwillingness to hold to a stated position. Simply stated, your visuals can help get across to your listener the idea that you have carefully thought out what you have to say, and to convince them that they will be safe to take what you say as *fact*.

Take advantage of these proven means to *SELL YOUR IDEA*.

HOW TO SHOW AN OBJECT

Nothing is more real, or can demonstrate a particular object in your speech better than the object itself. For instance you might be showing the advantages of a new cigarette lighter, or the new design of a compact, more efficient package.

Nothing can tell your story as well as *the* lighter or *the* package. Show it.

But show it right!

Here are some rules than can help your demonstration of an object:

——Be sure your audience can *see* everything you

point out on the object you hold. If they can't, you're going to have to enlarge that part by drawing a picture!

——Point to the part of the object you want the audience to concentrate on. Don't just wave it in front of them. One of the great strengths of using a physical object to support your speech is that this is an excellent way to *make* your audience *follow* you; they can't get ahead of you!

——Don't hold the object in front of you. If you do it will probably blend into your suit, tie or shirt. You want it to stand out for easy viewing by the audience. Hold it naturally, about shoulder level, approximately five inches from your body. Practice learning to handle objects without appearing awkward. It isn't difficult!

——Most important! If the device you're showing is supposed to *work*, be sure you know how to operate it. Nothing is more embarrassing to a speaker than being caught demonstrating an object and finding out in *front of his audience* that he doesn't really know its operation!

——Plan when you will pick up the object you're demonstrating. Then don't pick it up *until* that time! One of the audience's pet peeves is to have to watch a speaker who plays with a visual object but never seems to get to demonstrate it. These 'false' actions mislead as badly as words!

——If you decide to carry the object in your pocket, be sure you can find it when the time comes. Your author has seen literally dozens of speakers pull the famous (or infamous) act of the bridegroom who can't find the ring. In this situation, the audience has no mercy. And the speaker deserves none!

A speaker who wants to add immediate interest power to his business speaking can turn right away to the high octane of visual demonstration.

Try it in your next speech and see the difference!

HOW TO USE LINE AND BAR GRAPHS

Everyone understands that which they can see more quickly than something they hear. Psychologists point out that the eye is a much more effective instrument for gathering and storing information than the ear.

The reason is simple enough. Think for a minute how spoken words work; you have to add each word to the one that went before and finally you come up with the whole meaning. On the other hand, visuals present *all* the information at once. The eye can grasp the *whole* immediately.

The above is one reason why charts have become so important to business and industrial organizations. Numbers are a basic tool in business; the message they carry very often is the force that swings the balance, proves the point being made, in the end, determines company action.

However, numbers when presented in bulk, tend to work *against* themselves and lull, instead of stimulating, the thinking of the audience. This is where the value of the graph comes in!

For instance, graphs can present in a single viewing the complete growth or decline picture of the production

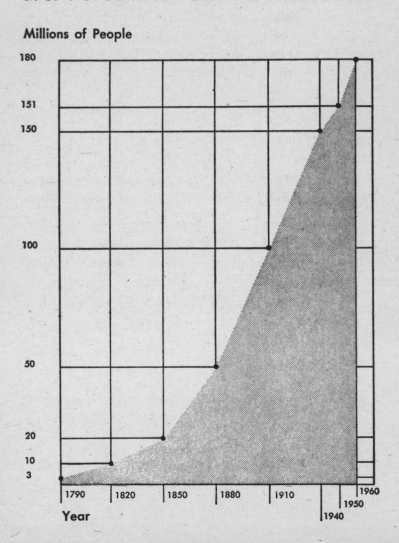

U. S. POPULATION GROWTH FROM 1790

Millions of People

trend you are describing. Or they can expose, in one presentation, the shipments of a product for the last year and compare them to sales quotas.

Here are several forms of graphs; note that each type has a particular strength; each one is particularly well-suited to do a special job.

The line graph can be used very effectively to present the visual idea of *rise or fall*, growth or decline, over a specified period. Perhaps, you wish to show the growth of population in the U. S. since the year 1790. The line graph could do this instantly!

When you use the line graph to prove your point, keep the following suggestions in mind:

——Always put a heading over the graph which spells out clearly what it is supposed to tell the audience.

——Be sure to label *both* legs of your graph . . . and be sure the labels are visible to your viewers!

——Label both legs of your graph horizontally . . . remember that your audience cannot pick up your graph and turn it around (as they would a page) for easy viewing!

——Draw your lines *definitely* so the last man in the last row can see easily. Nothing could be more useless than a visual that is not visible!

——If there are important points in your graph, mark them with arrows to pinpoint the attention of your viewers. Make it easy for them to learn; they're sure to appreciate it.

——Use color, it will always be one of the best and simplest way to attract and hold attention.

The bar graph is particularly well-suited to present immediate *comparisons* of like ideas, events or trends. For instance, if you wanted to show the size of the merchant fleets of the world, comparing the years 1939 and 1959, it would look like this on the bar graph:

MERCHANT FLEETS OF THE WORLD (GROSS TONS)

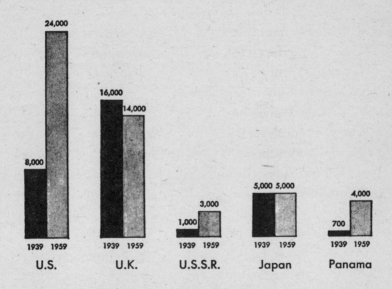

The bar graph may be used vertically or horizontally, whichever way best seems to present the information you are visualizing. Add these guides to the suggestions offered for use of the line graph:

——Place your designation *within* the bar when

possible. It will help translate the meaning of each bar quickly.

——Set off the growth of one bar over another by using color to spotlight the difference (see the illustration). This follows the basic rule of visuals; the quicker the audience understands, the better your chance of their believing what you have to say!

HOW TO USE A PICTOGRAPH

The pictograph is entering like a breath of fresh air into more and more visual presentations. By its use, thousands of grateful listeners are able instantly to receive and understand facts that would be dull as dust if presented in the usual form of statistical tables. An audience that is relaxed and happy is easy to talk to, easy on the speaker, and easier to convince!

The pictograph serves the goal stated by one of the most famous knights, scholar, teacher, soldier of the 16th century —Sir Philip Sidney. In outlining the best way to teach or persuade someone, he said: "It must be done in such a pleasant way as will draw in the children from play and the old men from the chimney corner."

In other words, he was saying, "Make what you have to say easy to understand, pleasant to learn, and your reward will be that people will remember it." The pictograph does this unusually well.

The pictograph is a symbolic presentation of the object or objects being described. For instance, you have probably seen the visual of a coin divided into parts to show how government spending is allocated to different departments.

Or, the use of silhouette soldiers to show the armed forces of a country. Or, a factory to show an industry. The pictograph is the most effective of visuals because it *visually translates* the idea for the viewer.

The pictograph gives an immediate *visual* comparison of the idea being presented. No translation of numbers, tables, graphs is needed; the audience can *see* and understand almost as soon as the visual is revealed. It is the *most* effective form of visual aid available to today's speaker. Take advantage of the pictograph and let it work for you.

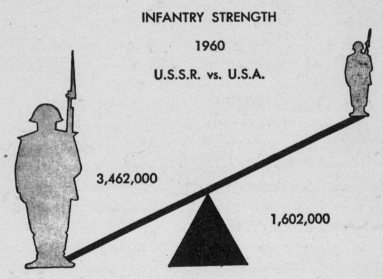

INFANTRY STRENGTH

1960

U.S.S.R. vs. U.S.A.

3,462,000

1,602,000

Here are some suggestions that will help make the pictograph work well:

——Make your picture as simple as possible. Detail drawings work *against* the simple and direct presentation of the idea.

——Make the picture symbols bear the major responsibility of making the idea clear. Any labels or numbers are only *extra* support. Set as a standard the guide that the picture could stand *alone* if necessary!

——The pictograph is frequently used to show comparisons. Heighten these comparisons by using color to define for the viewer how great the difference is.

Take full advantage of the pictograph whenever you have the chance. It stimulates as it informs; it interests as it teaches; it entertains as it supports your ideas. It is frequently the difference between the speech everyone talks about and the speech no one remembers (out of self-defense!).

Try the pictograph on your next audience . . . and then ask them for *their* opinion!

HOW TO USE A FLANNEL BOARD

Here is an excellent way to present a finished-looking demonstration that is easy to prepare, easy to use, with a device that never fails to interest and stimulate an audience. In addition to the fact that the flannel board has proved its communication value everytime it's been used, the novelty of the board makes it of even greater importance to your speaking. Chances are that your listeners may never have seen a flannel board used and as a visual aid technique it's bound to excite them!

Here is what the flannel board is and what it can do.

Flannel boards are pieces of plywood, fiberboard, masonite, etc., varying in size from 2' x 4' to 3' x 6' to larger, covered with a black flannel tightly drawn over the surface. On this black background you affix your charts, diagrams, and other prepared visuals.

You lay out your visuals on illustration paper; drawing the pictographs, diagrams, charts, statistics, etc., on whatever color background you prefer. When your visuals are finished, you paste pieces of sandpaper on the back (use the heaviest gauge sandpaper you can find, and paste in the corners).

As you give your speech, all you need do to exhibit your information is to press these visuals onto the flannel board. The roughness of the sandpaper will make them hold to the flannel. They'll stay there until you pick them off.

The flannel board allows you to develop and build an idea in front of your audience by laying it out as you talk. Listeners will never fail to be intrigued by this device that seems to defy gravity!

For those speakers who like their visuals in a more finished form, visual supply houses have colored and white paper designed specifically for flannel-board use with the holding surface already sprayed on the back. Whether you buy it or make it—try it! It will really pay off in successful speaking!

HOW TO USE CHARTS . . . THE BLACKBOARD

These two devices offer probably the most convenient and flexible means of visualizing ideas and supporting your speech. Thousands of teachers everyday depend on the blackboard to help them in their teaching. Charts have become a part of almost every well-developed speech in business. Both these visual techniques have their advantages and limitations.

CHARTS: Large white charts, either of heavy illustration paper or drawn on a common white pad can be very helpful in making your idea clear to the audience, since, as pointed out earlier, all listeners are more eye-minded than ear-minded. If your diagram is complicated you will probably want to prepare it completely *before* the speech. However, if the diagram is simple, it's often a good idea to develop it as you proceed. By the way, this technique is an excellent way of keeping the audience *with* you—keeping them from coming to the point *before* you make it!

Warning: Lay your diagrams out in an orderly fashion. Your audience has a long established habit of reading from left to right, top to bottom. It is foolhardy to try to break it now! Lay your material out in this familiar pattern and you will help your listener and viewer follow your material easily and rapidly. As with all other visual devices, use color and variety to stimulate interest. The one big weakness in charts is that everyone has seen them used many, many times before . . . and frequently used poorly. Nevertheless, well-drawn, simple and original charts can work very hard for you in supporting your speech.

BLACKBOARD: The blackboard is too often regarded as only a visual device for use in the classroom. The very reason it has such wide use in teaching is because it is one of the best ways of outlining and dramatizing a thought. You can see that few mediums give the flexibility of the blackboard; the ability to erase and present a new idea on the *same* surface time after time is a definite plus.

As with the chart, the blackboard speaker should take advantage of color to hypo interest and to get clearer definition of his idea.

Plan how you are going to use the blackboard and be sure you are writing firmly enough for *all* your audience to see. If you are in doubt, test your writing *before* the speech begins; after the speech begins, it's too late!

It's easy to develop a terrible jumble in laying out your material on the blackboard. Again, trade on the pattern viewers have of reading left to right and top to bottom. Lay your visuals out accordingly.

One last thought; don't work against the background of a cluttered blackboard. It's very distracting to your viewers. When you have finished with a diagram on the board, erase it and give the audience nothing to look at but *you!* That's the way it should be!

USING VISUAL PROJECTORS

Many scholars of language and communication have underlined the sharp difference between words and pictures; that words build one upon the next, that pictures present the whole idea at one time. This is a communication principle that good speakers have traded on for many years; using the picture to tell an immediate and vivid story.

Today, many new machines have been developed to make the presentation of visual ideas easier and even more dramatic than was possible a few years ago. These machines can be divided roughly into three types:

1. Motion picture projectors
2. Slide and strip projectors
3. Overhead projectors

Let's take a quick look at each and examine their strengths and weaknesses.

MOTION PICTURES: Here is an excellent way to present ideas in a very finished form. This type of presentation is made strong by the highly flexible flow of ideas; by the ability of the camera to move freely and easily from scene to scene, from place to place, providing a running audio track with the picture. Since we have all been brought up in the age of the "movies" and have always associated the movies with fun, they have a built-in appeal for all audiences.

Motion pictures can be successfully used to put vitality in your speech, but they have their limitations too. Limitations you must learn to recognize.

——Motion pictures demand a completely darkened room and a darkened room carries with it loss of attention and not infrequently sleep. When the lights go out, the speaker loses his identity and with it goes his control. If you use movies, try doing the commentary yourself and thereby draw the attention of the listener to yourself as speaker.

——Be sure the machine you use is in good working order. Nothing is more appalling than the visual device that won't operate; the projector that "worked just this afternoon." Audiences dislike amateurs; they don't expect Cinemascope, but they do expect something that works!

——Use the film to *support* your speech; don't let the picture *become* the speech. A good idea is to open your presentation orally and then use the movie to support the points you want to emphasize. Then close with a *GET ACTION* Step that ties up the purpose of the presentation and tells your listeners exactly what you want them to do. In other words, make the film a tool . . . *you* be the speaker, not the machine!

——Remember, your audience has probably seen their fill of "home movies" and has had the usual reaction. If you are going to use this film, you have to be *sure* it has the quality that makes it worth showing. Think of the poor viewer!

——Check carefully to determine where you can place your projector. More than one unfortunate speaker has planned to show films as the main support of his presentation only to find that the projector obscured a full fifty percent of his audience! Another great idea with the impact of a wet muffin!

——One last suggestion: Check the current. Is it AC or DC? Enough said!

SLIDE AND STRIP PROJECTORS: More and more people have taken to collecting pictures of their trips, etc., as a record of their pleasant family life. As a result, dozens of excellent slide projectors are on the market. today. Speakers have been quick to find that these same projectors are just the device to hammer home an idea in an entertaining way and with lasting effect. The strip projector which is now also being used widely, is simply a series of slides fastened together in a strip form on film.

Don't overlook the slide and strip film projector when you plan your next speech. And when you use it, keep these ideas in mind:

——As with the film projector, the slide projector must be used in a dark room; don't let it take over. Remember *you* are the speaker, not the machine.

——New slide and strip projectors have long cord attachments which allow the speaker to change his own slide frames. Use it! It avoids that tired old phrase to the much maligned machine operator, "May we have the next slide, please."

——Several new slide projectors are available with sound attachments that play a record in coordination with the slides or film strips. We would advise against them! There is no reason to replace the speaker with a mechanical device. If you do, the speaker may just as well stay at home and let the audience listen to a recording.

OVERHEAD PROJECTORS: Here is an excellent device (used unfortunately too little) which will add a professional touch to any speaker's presentation. Some of you may have seen these projectors used in bowling alleys; they are the machines that project the bowling score onto overhead screens.

Here's how the business speaker can use the overhead projector. Visuals are prepared on transparent sheets of acetate varying in size from 3" x 3" to 8" x 8". The acetate is placed on a polished glass surface of the projector through which a strong light shines. The light projects through the acetate picking up the illustration the speaker has made, passes up through an optical lens and is thrown forward onto a screen. The overhead projector is a natural for the speaker. Here are some of the reasons:

——The overhead projector can be used in a fully lighted room. This has always been the main trouble with other projecting devices; the fact that the speaker had to work in a darkened room and risk the chance that his audience would consider this a good opportunity for a quick cat nap!

——This type projector is easily portable.

——The speaker can easily prepare his own transparencies thus avoiding the considerable cost of professional slide preparation.

——The speaker can stand in a lighted room, face his audience, place the transparencies on the projector and have them thrown over his head on a screen. This means that the speaker always faces his audience and is in close personal control of the visual device. Very important!

——Overlays of different color transparencies can be used to show growth or change or comparison in your speech. The overhead projector gives the speaker flexibility in visual presentations not to be found in other devices.

Visual projectors can make *any* speech better! Look up your nearest visual aid distributor and ask him to show you what is available for you as a speaker.

MORE VISUAL AID EQUIPMENT

Here are some additional visual aid materials you should be familiar with and consider for use in the next important presentation you are called upon to give. If you use them well, you'll have a big jump on the problem of giving a good speech; a speech that will show your ability and intelligence; a speech that will communicate clearly and convince people it is logical to do what you suggest.

Crayons   Get several in a variety of colors for use in developing charts, diagrams, graphs, etc. Look for a heavy crayon that will make a broad, definite line on your paper.

Chalk   If you use a blackboard (you should try it), don't forget color. Try definite colors (red, yellow, green, blue, as well as white), since these colors will be most visible and will add interest and clarity to the ideas you present.

Plastic Tapes   Several manufacturers now produce plastic tapes (packaged like mending tapes) of various widths and colors which are a natural for laying out bar and line graphs. Just label your base and then strip off the color tape you need and the visual is done! A real boon for the speaker!

Ink Markers   Many businessmen do not have the services of a professional artist to call on when a visual is needed. Most have to do the work themselves. Very often, these people are self-conscious about their drawing ability and their ability to letter a diagram. There are now on the market several ink markers which demand nothing more than taking off the top of the marker and drawing the line. With these markers, *everyone* can produce a thoroughly acceptable visual presentation.

Color Transparencies   Sheets of transparent paper in a multitude of shades are available in most art stores for use as overlays in the visual presentation of an idea. The way to use them is to draw the basic visual and then use these overlays to further develop or expand the basic idea. This is an excellent way to show the development of a plant, growth in sales, change in package design, etc. Try this in your next speech; chances are your audience has never seen this device used before!

There is one request all audiences constantly ask and which visuals constantly fulfill. The request is "Show Me!"

EXERCISES. . . .

The visuals you will use in your next speech will, of course be tailored to that particular speech. Just set a goal for yourself to *use* visuals in your next speech! In addition, do the following . . .

1. Make a definite effort to get to know the visual aids available to you in your company. Get to know them *personally*. Touch them, try them.

2. Visit your nearest art store and look over the materials they have that you could use. Like plastic tapes of different widths, colored paper, etc. Go now, you will have better ideas of visuals for your next speech.

3. Look over the next speech you are asked to give. See where a visual will help to make your ideas clearer. Be sure to examine the different ways to visualize the point. Don't settle for one way because it's easier.

4. Be sure to work *with* your visual aids. Don't stand back from them. Walk up to them and point out what you want the listeners to understand. Practice working with your visuals, you will find that this familiarity will help you when your audience is sitting in front of you.

One Final Review

As SPEAKER, all your efforts up to this point have been to present your ideas in a dramatic and memorable fashion in order to win the acceptance and agreement of your audience. This book has suggested that the "good" speeches are given by forceful speakers who present their ideas in a logical and orderly pattern; a pattern that answers the questions and doubts of the audience as they arise. We have called this pattern the "Outline to Direct Talk." It is *the* most important road map to good speaking anyone can offer to you. If you use it, you will become one of the better speakers in your organization!

Let's look at this Outline one more time:

COMMAND YOUR AUDIENCE
(Purpose: To get attention; to stimulate interest; to

help the speaker to meet his audience; to prepare the audience for the "meat" of your speech.)

DIRECT YOUR FIRE

(Purpose: To bring the subject over to your audience; to make it the personal responsibility of *this* audience; to point up the importance of the subject.)

SAY WHAT YOU MEAN

(Purpose: To state the theme of your speech exactly; to be sure the audience knows where you stand and what you are going to expand on and prove.)

SELL YOUR IDEA

(Purpose: To expand on your central theme; to prove the point you have made to your listeners.)

At this point your speech is finished. You have stated your point and you have given the necessary information to support your position. Your ideas must now stand on their own merits. You have had *full* opportunity to prove your point.

However, one very important job remains to be done. You must tell the listener just what he is to *do* with the information you have offered. You, as speaker, must fulfill one final step . . . *to get action.*

Get Action

THE ONLY good speech is the one that points out to the audience just what the audience is to do with the information it has been given; just what action they are expected to take. Even more important, the good speech tells the audience *how* to take that action.

The final step of the Outline for Direct Talk is the one that brings the results! It is the pay-off!

When a member of the Fire Department comes to your door to ask you to come to the town Fire Department dance, he gets action by pulling out his pad and offering you a ticket.

When you go to your local auto dealer to look at a car, the dealer explains the features of the car, then points out why this makes it a better car to own, *then* tells you how you can pay for it—either in cash, or by a loan. And he has the forms right there!

The business speaker who has an idea to present, ends by pointing out to his listeners *exactly* what is needed from them to put the idea he has proposed into effect.

A speech without a good *GET ACTION* Step is often a big build-up to . . . nothing! You may have your listeners nodding, but there is a great difference between agreement and the physical action that is needed to make the plan a working one.

Be sure you end your speech with a firm conclusion; a conclusion that will make your audience walk out determined to see that the next step in the plan goes into the works *immediately*.

Think about these suggestions when you come to close your next speech:

1. *Always* tell *every* audience what you want them them to do with the information you have presented in your speech. The speech may have been long and it's easy for the listener to become lulled by the sound of your voice. Do him a favor, give him new "directions."

2. Explain very carefully *how* they can apply the information you have presented. For instance, if you have been convincing them they *should* give blood, tell them *where*. And make it sound easy to get there! The enthusiasm of the audience frequently fades quickly, and your stimulus is most important.

3. If you were simply presenting ideas that you want your listeners to mull over, *tell* them this is what

you want them to do. Again, make it easy for them to get the ideas straight by summarizing the important thoughts in the order of their importance. This will give the audience a pocket digest they can take out the door of the meeting room.

4. Try to end on a high note that emphasizes the value of doing what the speaker asks. Appeal to the higher motives of the listener. Call on the dramatic effect of the vital and inspirational words in our language; put them together to *GET ACTION!*

Here is an example of a good solid inspirational ending which closes the speech of Mr. Clarence E. Manion, former Chairman of the Commission on Intergovernmental Relations:

"Will you think about that please, the next time you pay that life insurance premium, the next time you review that will, the next time you stash away a few dollars in the bank? Please think of it, my friends. Think hard about it. Do you want to do something about it? Then gather those youngsters around you and look them in the eye, as I have looked at mine. Then and there you will make a resolution. God helping you a little, you will then and there be resolved that your legacy—not of property, but of liberty—to those youngsters is going to compare favorably with the big fortune of freedom which the Founding Fathers left to you."

Your speech is complete.

How to Prepare for Your Next Speech

ALL THE IDEAS of this book were directed to one goal . . . to help you make your next speech a good one. The authority for these ideas comes from the fact that they have been distilled from the problems and proficiencies of literally thousands of speakers, all of whom experienced the same feelings of inadequacy and insecurity common to all people who find they must stand before their fellow humans and present an idea.

All the information you need to make your next speech a really good one has been presented in the pages you have read. The use of this information must rest with you.

In order to promote this use, the author offers one more guide . . . a guide to lead the speaker through the preparation of his upcoming speech, from the first time he gets his subject to that satisfying moment when the audience offers him their full approval.

The development of a speech which will satisfy listeners is not difficult, but it does demand two things. One is physical—careful preparation, the other psychological—the desire to do a good job and the feeling that you will. This is a combination you can't beat.

For the sake of an imaginary situation, let's assume you have just been asked by the President of the 4 A's (American Association of Advertising Agencies) to make a speech on "something to do with advertising in today's business."

This subject is just about as vague as those most speakers are confronted with!

You have three weeks to prepare for this speech, which presents you with the choice of one of two ways to proceed. You can wait until two days before the meeting before starting to prepare and thus settle for a poor performance OR you can start work immediately, choose your subject and do a job that everyone will recognize as a top rank.

We must assume that you are a rational being and that you will choose the latter; that you are convinced that you were chosen to make this particular speech because everyone believed you have something important to say, and that this faith in you deserves careful preparation. Add to this the effect this speech can have on your relationships with your colleagues and the stimulus it can have on your career.

This goal is certainly worth a well thought-out effort.

The following is a guide to the development of your presentation . . . follow it step by step!

CHOOSING THE SUBJECT

You will note that the subject for your hypothetical speech before the 4 A's was "something to do with advertising in today's business." This is about as definite as betting on a horse! But don't blame the toastmaster. He hesitates about being *too* specific, feeling, no doubt, that the speaker should be allowed to make the decision as to his exact subject. Your first job then is to make this decision.

Set a time limit for yourself to decide upon the exact subject for your speech. The time limit can vary with the amount of time you have before you must give your speech, but try to decide within two days of getting your assignment. *Warning:* Live by your two-day schedule to make your subject final. Too many speakers vacillate uncertainly at this step in the preparation and end up wasting valuable time; time that can't be made up. Don't hesitate . . . think of possible subjects, then decide!

When you have your subject, *word it* as you will use it in your central theme; the step we have called in our outline the *SAY WHAT YOU MEAN* Step. Now you are ready to begin your actual preparation.

One last suggestion on your choice of a subject, if you are a guest speaker, call your toastmaster and tell him what it is. This will keep you from wasting time on a subject the toastmaster may feel is not exactly on target, or if he likes it, will help him develop his introduction of you to the audience.

BEGINNING PREPARATION

With your subject clearly in mind, pick up about six

3" x 5" white cards at your stationers. You will use these cards in outlining your speech, and they will serve as cue cards when you deliver it.

Type or write the Outline for Direct Talk on the upper left corner of the cards.

For instance, card #1 will read *COMMAND YOUR AUDIENCE*; card #2, *DIRECT YOUR FIRE*; card #3, *SAY WHAT YOU MEAN*; cards #4 and #5, *SELL YOUR IDEA*; and card #6, *GET ACTION*. Thus each card will be a guide through the material of your speech. With the outline on the cards to lead you, you can't possibly get off the track. You can then devote all your attention to making your speech direct and sharp!

FIRST DEVELOPMENT STEP

Now start with card #3, *SAY WHAT YOU MEAN*, and *write out* the central theme of your speech. The reason for this procedure is that many speakers find that if they start at the top of the speech, i.e. the *COMMAND YOUR AUDIENCE* Step, they are already off the track by the time they reach the central theme. Starting your outline with the *SAY WHAT YOU MEAN* Step will keep you from wandering off on a tangent.

SECOND DEVELOPMENT STEP

You are now ready to take cards 4 & 5 and to put down all the proof, examples, contrasts, stories, figures, statistics, logic, visuals, etc. that will *SELL YOUR IDEA*. There are two ways to set up your cue cards, by writing out the *exact* words you plan to use in each step OR by writing out the *ideas* in sentence form. Both methods work; use the one you like best.

Remember, however, the strength of your *SELL YOUR IDEA* support will probably determine the selling power of your whole speech. Give it the time and care of preparation it deserves!

THIRD DEVELOPMENT STEP

You are now ready to take card #6 and set down your plea for audience action. Tell your listeners what you want them to do and tell them *how* they can do it.

It is a good idea to *write out* the final sentence of your speech *completely*. Then memorize it. This is the last chance you will have with your audience and you want to be sure you end on a strong note!

FOURTH DEVELOPMENT STEP

At this point, go back to card #1 and develop a hard-hitting, vital, attention-getting opening. Remember, you must make this *COMMAND YOUR AUDIENCE* Step tie in with your speech, so choose an opening that will lead logically into the theme that follows.

FIFTH DEVELOPMENT STEP

Take card #2 (*DIRECT YOUR FIRE*) and write the sentence that will bring the subject down to *this* audience. If you have gotten attention with your *COMMAND* Step, this Step will make your ideas the personal business of everyone listening.

WORDING YOUR SPEECH

The direct line of your speech has now been set down

in outline form. There should be no reason for your reasoning to swerve off the logical path of your ideas.

Your next job is to word your ideas as dramatically and vitally as you can. Again, you may proceed in several ways. Most speakers build their speech orally, directly from their cards. They prefer to "speak" the speech a number of times until the words begin to fall into place; until they use the same words each time they practice it. There are other speakers who prefer to write out the speech at this stage, working directly from their cards. When they have learned the speech, they throw the written sheets away and go back to the cue cards.

The written speech should never be read; the only exception is if you *know* the speech so well that you only turn to the script to pick up your ideas, *not* your words. Few people doubt that the speech that is read is a weak one!

PRACTICING YOUR SPEECH

How much you as speaker should practice depends on your aptitude in remembering your wording, etc. You should go completely through your presentation at least six times. At this point, take an appraisal to see if you need additional practice. Deliver your speech on your feet; if you can gather an audience (family, friends, etc.), do so.

Whatever you do, be *sure* to make your speech practice complete; imagine each practice session is the real thing. Your final presentation will show your effort.

1. Sit down and list five subjects, i.e. "Age has nothing to do with ability." Or, "We should withdraw all our troops from around the world." Or, "We should have reduced air fares for

adults, not kids."

2. Now take *one* of these subjects and lay out your speech on your 3x5 cards. Follow your Outline for Direct Talk carefully.

3. When you get to the Sell Your Idea step, be sure you develop at least a half dozen reasons why someone should believe you. Also, mix up your support. Use fact, quote, comparison, story, reason. Try to work in a visual or two.

4. Now work on the wording of your speech. Try to keep within a five to ten minute time limit. Try working from 'lead-in' ideas. Don't write your speech out, just clue yourself in.

5. Now stand up and practice at least five times all the way through. Aloud! Notice how much easier it gets each time.

6. Now try to get an audience for your effort. Family, kids, will do.

7. Go at it!

Now take the rest of your subjects one at a time and do the same on weekly intervals. You will be surprised to see how much you improve.

There is no other way!

In Closing

AT THIS POINT, this book ceases to be the presenter, and you take over as the speaker. The information you have read has been developed from practical work with practical people who discovered the single most important thing they had to do was to speak their ideas.

The ideas contained in this book worked for them—they will work for you.

You have all the information you need to be a *superior* speaker. If you use it, your decision to read this book can be the most important you have ever made.